I0037432

FLORIDA EVIDENCE CODE
2023 Edition

Updated through January 1, 2023

Michigan Legal Publishing Ltd.
QUICK DESK REFERENCE SERIES™

WE WELCOME YOUR FEEDBACK: info@michlp.com

ISBN-13: 978-1-64002-142-6

Table of Contents

Chapter 90 – Evidence Code

§ 90.101. Short title

This chapter shall be known and may be cited as the "Florida Evidence Code."

§ 90.102. Construction

This chapter shall replace and supersede existing statutory or common law in conflict with its provisions.

§ 90.103. Scope; applicability

(1) Unless otherwise provided by statute, this code applies to the same proceedings that the general law of evidence applied to before the effective date of this code.
(2) This act shall apply to criminal proceedings related to crimes committed after the effective date of this code and to civil actions and all other proceedings pending on or brought after October 1, 1981.
(3) Nothing in this act shall operate to repeal or modify the parol evidence rule.

§ 90.104. Rulings on evidence

(1) A court may predicate error, set aside or reverse a judgment, or grant a new trial on the basis of admitted or excluded evidence when a substantial right of the party is adversely affected and:
  (a) When the ruling is one admitting evidence, a timely objection or motion to strike appears on the record, stating the specific ground of objection if the specific ground was not apparent from the context; or
  (b) When the ruling is one excluding evidence, the substance of the evidence was made known to the court by offer of proof or was apparent from the context within which the questions were asked.
  If the court has made a definitive ruling on the record admitting or excluding evidence, either at or before trial, a party need not renew an objection or offer of proof to preserve a claim of error for appeal.
(2) In cases tried by a jury, a court shall conduct proceedings, to the maximum extent practicable, in such a manner as to prevent inadmissible evidence from being suggested to the jury by any means.

(3) Nothing in this section shall preclude a court from taking notice of fundamental errors affecting substantial rights, even though such errors were not brought to the attention of the trial judge.

§ 90.105. Preliminary questions

(1) Except as provided in subsection (2), the court shall determine preliminary questions concerning the qualification of a person to be a witness, the existence of a privilege, or the admissibility of evidence.

(2) When the relevancy of evidence depends upon the existence of a preliminary fact, the court shall admit the proffered evidence when there is prima facie evidence sufficient to support a finding of the preliminary fact. If prima facie evidence is not introduced to support a finding of the preliminary fact, the court may admit the proffered evidence subject to the subsequent introduction of prima facie evidence of the preliminary fact.

(3) Hearings on the admissibility of confessions shall be conducted out of the hearing of the jury. Hearings on other preliminary matters shall be similarly conducted when the interests of justice require or when an accused is a witness, if he or she so requests.

§ 90.106. Summing up and comment by judge

A judge may not sum up the evidence or comment to the jury upon the weight of the evidence, the credibility of the witnesses, or the guilt of the accused.

§ 90.107. Limited admissibility

When evidence that is admissible as to one party or for one purpose, but inadmissible as to another party or for another purpose, is admitted, the court, upon request, shall restrict such evidence to its proper scope and so inform the jury at the time it is admitted.

§ 90.108. Introduction of related writings or recorded statements

(1) When a writing or recorded statement or part thereof is introduced by a party, an adverse party may require him or her at that time to introduce any other part or any other writing or recorded statement that in fairness ought to be considered contemporaneously. An adverse party is not bound by evidence introduced under this section.

(2) The report of a court reporter, when certified to by the court reporter as being a correct transcript of the testimony and proceedings in the case, is prima facie a correct statement of such testimony and proceedings.

§ 90.201. Matters which must be judicially noticed

A court shall take judicial notice of:

(1) Decisional, constitutional, and public statutory law and resolutions of the Florida Legislature and the Congress of the United States.

(2) Florida rules of court that have statewide application, its own rules, and the rules of United States courts adopted by the United States Supreme Court.

(3) Rules of court of the United States Supreme Court and of the United States Courts of Appeal.

§ 90.202. Matters which may be judicially noticed

A court may take judicial notice of the following matters, to the extent that they are not embraced within s. 90.201:

(1) Special, local, and private acts and resolutions of the Congress of the United States and of the Florida Legislature.

(2) Decisional, constitutional, and public statutory law of every other state, territory, and jurisdiction of the United States.

(3) Contents of the Federal Register.

(4) Laws of foreign nations and of an organization of nations.

(5) Official actions of the legislative, executive, and judicial departments of the United States and of any state, territory, or jurisdiction of the United States.

(6) Records of any court of this state or of any court of record of the United States or of any state, territory, or jurisdiction of the United States.

(7) Rules of court of any court of this state or of any court of record of the United States or of any other state, territory, or jurisdiction of the United States.

(8) Provisions of all municipal and county charters and charter amendments of this state, provided they are available in printed copies or as certified copies.

(9) Rules promulgated by governmental agencies of this state which are published in the Florida Administrative Code or in bound written copies.

(10) Duly enacted ordinances and resolutions of municipalities and counties located in Florida, provided such ordinances and resolutions are available in printed copies or as certified copies.

(11) Facts that are not subject to dispute because they are generally known within the territorial jurisdiction of the court.

(12) Facts that are not subject to dispute because they are capable of accurate and ready determination by resort to sources whose accuracy cannot be questioned.

(13) Official seals of governmental agencies and departments of the United States and of any state, territory, or jurisdiction of the United States.

§ 90.203. Compulsory judicial notice upon request

A court shall take judicial notice of any matter in s. 90.202 when a party requests it and:

(1) Gives each adverse party timely written notice of the request, proof of which is filed with the court, to enable the adverse party to prepare to meet the request.

(2) Furnishes the court with sufficient information to enable it to take judicial notice of the matter.

§ 90.2035. Judicial notice of information taken from web mapping services, global satellite imaging sites, or Internet mapping tools

(1)

   (a) Upon request of a party, a court may take judicial notice of an image, map, location, distance, calculation, or other information taken from a widely accepted web mapping service, global satellite imaging site, or Internet mapping tool, if such image, map, location, distance, calculation, or other information indicates the date on which the information was created.

   (b) A party intending to offer such information in evidence at trial or at a hearing must file notice of such intent within a reasonable time or as defined by court order. The notice must include a copy of the information and specify the Internet address or pathway where such information may be accessed and inspected.

(2)

   (a) A party may object to the court taking judicial notice of the image, map, location, distance, calculation, or other information taken from a widely accepted web mapping service, global satellite imaging site, or Internet mapping tool within a reasonable time or as defined by court order.

(b) In civil cases, there is a rebuttable presumption that information sought to be judicially noticed under this section should be judicially noticed. The rebuttable presumption may be overcome if the court finds by the greater weight of the evidence that the information does not fairly and accurately portray what it is being offered to prove or that it otherwise should not be admitted into evidence under the Florida Evidence Code.

(c) If the court overrules the objection, the court must take judicial notice of the information and admit the information into evidence.

(3) In criminal cases, the court must instruct the jury that the jury may or may not accept the noticed facts as conclusive.

(4) This section does not affect, expand, or limit standards for any matters that may otherwise be judicially noticed.

§ 90.204. Determination of propriety of judicial notice and nature of matter noticed

(1) When a court determines upon its own motion that judicial notice of a matter should be taken or when a party requests such notice and shows good cause for not complying with s. 90.203(1), the court shall afford each party reasonable opportunity to present information relevant to the propriety of taking judicial notice and to the nature of the matter noticed.

(2) In determining the propriety of taking judicial notice of a matter or the nature thereof, a court may use any source of pertinent and reliable information, whether or not furnished by a party, without regard to any exclusionary rule except a valid claim of privilege and except for the exclusions provided in s. 90.403.

(3) If a court resorts to any documentary source of information not received in open court, the court shall make the information and its source a part of the record in the action and shall afford each party reasonable opportunity to challenge such information, and to offer additional information, before judicial notice of the matter is taken.

(4) In family cases, the court may take judicial notice of any matter described in s. 90.202(6) when imminent danger to persons or property has been alleged and it is impractical to give prior notice to the parties of the intent to take judicial notice. Opportunity to present evidence relevant to the propriety of taking judicial notice under subsection (1)

may be deferred until after judicial action has been taken. If judicial notice is taken under this subsection, the court shall, within 2 business days, file a notice in the pending case of the matters judicially noticed. For purposes of this subsection, the term "family cases" has the same meaning as provided in the Rules of Judicial Administration.

§ 90.205. Denial of a request for judicial notice

Upon request of counsel, when a court denies a request to take judicial notice of any matter, the court shall inform the parties at the earliest practicable time and shall indicate for the record that it has denied the request.

§ 90.206. Instructing jury on judicial notice

The court may instruct the jury during the trial to accept as a fact a matter judicially noticed.

§ 90.207. Judicial notice by trial court in subsequent proceedings

The failure or refusal of a court to take judicial notice of a matter does not preclude a court from taking judicial notice of the matter in subsequent proceedings, in accordance with the procedure specified in ss. 90.201-90.206.

§ 90.301. Presumption defined; inferences

(1) For the purposes of this chapter, a presumption is an assumption of fact which the law makes from the existence of another fact or group of facts found or otherwise established.
(2) Except for presumptions that are conclusive under the law from which they arise, a presumption is rebuttable.
(3) Nothing in this chapter shall prevent the drawing of an inference that is appropriate.
(4) Sections 90.301-90.304 are applicable only in civil actions or proceedings.

§ 90.302. Classification of rebuttable presumptions

Every rebuttable presumption is either:

(1) A presumption affecting the burden of producing evidence and requiring the trier of fact to assume the existence of the presumed fact, unless credible evidence sufficient to sustain a finding of the nonexistence of the presumed fact is introduced, in which event, the existence or nonexistence of the presumed fact shall be determined from the evidence without regard to the presumption; or

(2) A presumption affecting the burden of proof that imposes upon the party against whom it operates the burden of proof concerning the nonexistence of the presumed fact.

§ 90.303. Presumption affecting the burden of producing evidence defined

In a civil action or proceeding, unless otherwise provided by statute, a presumption established primarily to facilitate the determination of the particular action in which the presumption is applied, rather than to implement public policy, is a presumption affecting the burden of producing evidence.

§ 90.304. Presumption affecting the burden of proof defined

In civil actions, all rebuttable presumptions which are not defined in s. 90.303 are presumptions affecting the burden of proof.

§ 90.401. Definition of relevant evidence

Relevant evidence is evidence tending to prove or disprove a material fact.

§ 90.402. Admissibility of relevant evidence

All relevant evidence is admissible, except as provided by law.

§ 90.4025. Admissibility of paternity determination in certain criminal prosecutions

If a person less than 18 years of age gives birth to a child and the paternity of that child is established under chapter 742, such evidence of paternity is admissible in a criminal prosecution under ss. 794.011, 794.05, 800.04, and 827.04(3).

§ 90.4026. Statements expressing sympathy; admissibility; definitions

(1) As used in this section:
    (a) "Accident" means an occurrence resulting in injury or death to one or more persons which is not the result of willful action by a party.
    (b) "Benevolent gestures" means actions that convey a sense of compassion or commiseration emanating from human impulses.
    (c) "Family" means the spouse, parent, grandparent, stepmother, stepfather, child, grandchild, brother, sister, half-brother, half-sister, adopted child of parent, or spouse's parent of an injured party.

(2) The portion of statements, writings, or benevolent gestures expressing sympathy or a general sense of benevolence relating to the pain, suffering, or death of a person involved in an accident and made to that person or to the family of that person shall be inadmissible as evidence in a civil action. A statement of fault, however, which is part of, or in addition to, any of the above shall be admissible pursuant to this section.

§ 90.403. Exclusion on grounds of prejudice or confusion

Relevant evidence is inadmissible if its probative value is substantially outweighed by the danger of unfair prejudice, confusion of issues, misleading the jury, or needless presentation of cumulative evidence. This section shall not be construed to mean that evidence of the existence of available third-party benefits is inadmissible.

§ 90.404. Character evidence; when admissible

(1) **Character Evidence Generally**. Evidence of a person's character or a trait of character is inadmissible to prove action in conformity with it on a particular occasion, except:
    (a) *Character of accused*. Evidence of a pertinent trait of character offered by an accused, or by the prosecution to rebut the trait.
    (b) *Character of victim*.
        1. Except as provided in s. 794.022, evidence of a pertinent trait of character of the victim of the crime offered by an accused, or by the prosecution to rebut the trait; or

2. Evidence of a character trait of peacefulness of the victim offered by the prosecution in a homicide case to rebut evidence that the victim was the aggressor.

(c) *Character of witness*. Evidence of the character of a witness, as provided in ss. 90.608-90.610.

(2) **Other Crimes, Wrongs, or Acts**.

(a) Similar fact evidence of other crimes, wrongs, or acts is admissible when relevant to prove a material fact in issue, including, but not limited to, proof of motive, opportunity, intent, preparation, plan, knowledge, identity, or absence of mistake or accident, but it is inadmissible when the evidence is relevant solely to prove bad character or propensity.

(b)

1. In a criminal case in which the defendant is charged with a crime involving child molestation, evidence of the defendant's commission of other crimes, wrongs, or acts of child molestation is admissible and may be considered for its bearing on any matter to which it is relevant.

2. For the purposes of this paragraph, the term "child molestation" means conduct proscribed by s. 787.025(2)(c), s. 787.06(3)(g), former s. 787.06(3)(h), s. 794.011, excluding s. 794.011(10), s. 794.05, former s. 796.03, former s. 796.035, s. 800.04, s. 827.071, s. 847.0135(5), s. 847.0145, or s. 985.701(1) when committed against a person 16 years of age or younger.

(c)

1. In a criminal case in which the defendant is charged with a sexual offense, evidence of the defendant's commission of other crimes, wrongs, or acts involving a sexual offense is admissible and may be considered for its bearing on any matter to which it is relevant.

2. For the purposes of this paragraph, the term "sexual offense" means conduct proscribed by s. 787.025(2)(c), s. 787.06(3)(b), (d), (f), or (g), former s. 787.06(3)(h), s. 794.011, excluding s. 794.011(10), s. 794.05, former s. 796.03, former s. 796.035, s. 825.1025(2)(b), s. 827.071, s. 847.0135(5), s. 847.0145, or s. 985.701(1).

(d)

1. When the state in a criminal action intends to offer evidence of other criminal offenses under paragraph (a), paragraph (b),

or paragraph (c), no fewer than 10 days before trial, the state shall furnish to the defendant or to the defendant's counsel a written statement of the acts or offenses it intends to offer, describing them with the particularity required of an indictment or information. No notice is required for evidence of offenses used for impeachment or on rebuttal.

2. When the evidence is admitted, the court shall, if requested, charge the jury on the limited purpose for which the evidence is received and is to be considered. After the close of the evidence, the jury shall be instructed on the limited purpose for which the evidence was received and that the defendant cannot be convicted for a charge not included in the indictment or information.

(3) Nothing in this section affects the admissibility of evidence under s. 90.610.

§ 90.405. Methods of proving character

(1) **Reputation**. When evidence of the character of a person or of a trait of that person's character is admissible, proof may be made by testimony about that person's reputation.

(2) **Specific Instances of Conduct**. When character or a trait of character of a person is an essential element of a charge, claim, or defense, proof may be made of specific instances of that person's conduct.

§ 90.406. Routine practice

Evidence of the routine practice of an organization, whether corroborated or not and regardless of the presence of eyewitnesses, is admissible to prove that the conduct of the organization on a particular occasion was in conformity with the routine practice.

§ 90.407. Subsequent remedial measures

Evidence of measures taken after an injury or harm caused by an event, which measures if taken before the event would have made injury or harm less likely to occur, is not admissible to prove negligence, the existence of a product defect, or culpable conduct in connection with the event. This rule does not require the exclusion of evidence of subsequent remedial measures when offered for another purpose, such as proving ownership, control, or the feasibility of precautionary measures, if controverted, or impeachment.

§ 90.408. Compromise and offers to compromise

Evidence of an offer to compromise a claim which was disputed as to validity or amount, as well as any relevant conduct or statements made in negotiations concerning a compromise, is inadmissible to prove liability or absence of liability for the claim or its value.

§ 90.409. Payment of medical and similar expenses

Evidence of furnishing, or offering or promising to pay, medical or hospital expenses or other damages occasioned by an injury or accident is inadmissible to prove liability for the injury or accident.

§ 90.410. Offer to plead guilty; nolo contendere; withdrawn pleas of guilty

Evidence of a plea of guilty, later withdrawn; a plea of nolo contendere; or an offer to plead guilty or nolo contendere to the crime charged or any other crime is inadmissible in any civil or criminal proceeding. Evidence of statements made in connection with any of the pleas or offers is inadmissible, except when such statements are offered in a prosecution under chapter 837.

§ 90.501. Privileges recognized only as provided

Except as otherwise provided by this chapter, any other statute, or the Constitution of the United States or of the State of Florida, no person in a legal proceeding has a privilege to:
(1) Refuse to be a witness.
(2) Refuse to disclose any matter.
(3) Refuse to produce any object or writing.
(4) Prevent another from being a witness, from disclosing any matter, or from producing any object or writing.

§ 90.5015. Journalist's privilege

(1) **Definitions**. For purposes of this section, the term:
    (a) "Professional journalist" means a person regularly engaged in collecting, photographing, recording, writing, editing, reporting,

or publishing news, for gain or livelihood, who obtained the information sought while working as a salaried employee of, or independent contractor for, a newspaper, news journal, news agency, press association, wire service, radio or television station, network, or news magazine. Book authors and others who are not professional journalists, as defined in this paragraph, are not included in the provisions of this section.

(b) "News" means information of public concern relating to local, statewide, national, or worldwide issues or events.

(2) **Privilege**. A professional journalist has a qualified privilege not to be a witness concerning, and not to disclose the information, including the identity of any source, that the professional journalist has obtained while actively gathering news. This privilege applies only to information or eyewitness observations obtained within the normal scope of employment and does not apply to physical evidence, eyewitness observations, or visual or audio recording of crimes. A party seeking to overcome this privilege must make a clear and specific showing that:

(a) The information is relevant and material to unresolved issues that have been raised in the proceeding for which the information is sought;

(b) The information cannot be obtained from alternative sources; and

(c) A compelling interest exists for requiring disclosure of the information.

(3) **Disclosure**. A court shall order disclosure pursuant to subsection (2) only of that portion of the information for which the showing under subsection (2) has been made and shall support such order with clear and specific findings made after a hearing.

(4) **Waiver**. A professional journalist does not waive the privilege by publishing or broadcasting information.

(5) **Construction**. This section must not be construed to limit any privilege or right provided to a professional journalist under law.

(6) **Authentication**. Photographs, diagrams, video recordings, audio recordings, computer records, or other business records maintained, disclosed, provided, or produced by a professional journalist, or by the employer or principal of a professional journalist, may be authenticated for admission in evidence upon a showing, by affidavit of the professional journalist, or other individual with personal knowledge, that the photograph, diagram, video recording, audio recording, computer record, or other business record is a true and

accurate copy of the original, and that the copy truly and accurately reflects the observations and facts contained therein.

(7) **Accuracy of Evidence**. If the affidavit of authenticity and accuracy, or other relevant factual circumstance, causes the court to have clear and convincing doubts as to the authenticity or accuracy of the proferred evidence, the court may decline to admit such evidence.

(8) **Severability**. If any provision of this section or its application to any particular person or circumstance is held invalid, that provision or its application is severable and does not affect the validity of other provisions or applications of this section.

§ 90.502. Lawyer-client privilege

(1) For purposes of this section:
   (a) A "lawyer" is a person authorized, or reasonably believed by the client to be authorized, to practice law in any state or nation.
   (b) A "client" is any person, public officer, corporation, association, or other organization or entity, either public or private, who consults a lawyer with the purpose of obtaining legal services or who is rendered legal services by a lawyer.
   (c) A communication between lawyer and client is "confidential" if it is not intended to be disclosed to third persons other than:
      1. Those to whom disclosure is in furtherance of the rendition of legal services to the client.
      2. Those reasonably necessary for the transmission of the communication.

(2) A client has a privilege to refuse to disclose, and to prevent any other person from disclosing, the contents of confidential communications when such other person learned of the communications because they were made in the rendition of legal services to the client.

(3) The privilege may be claimed by:
   (a) The client.
   (b) A guardian or conservator of the client.
   (c) The personal representative of a deceased client.
   (d) A successor, assignee, trustee in dissolution, or any similar representative of an organization, corporation, or association or other entity, either public or private, whether or not in existence.
   (e) The lawyer, but only on behalf of the client. The lawyer's authority to claim the privilege is presumed in the absence of contrary evidence.

(4) There is no lawyer-client privilege under this section when:

    (a) The services of the lawyer were sought or obtained to enable or aid anyone to commit or plan to commit what the client knew was a crime or fraud.

    (b) A communication is relevant to an issue between parties who claim through the same deceased client.

    (c) A communication is relevant to an issue of breach of duty by the lawyer to the client or by the client to the lawyer, arising from the lawyer-client relationship.

    (d) A communication is relevant to an issue concerning the intention or competence of a client executing an attested document to which the lawyer is an attesting witness, or concerning the execution or attestation of the document.

    (e) A communication is relevant to a matter of common interest between two or more clients, or their successors in interest, if the communication was made by any of them to a lawyer retained or consulted in common when offered in a civil action between the clients or their successors in interest.

(5) Communications made by a person who seeks or receives services from the Department of Revenue under the child support enforcement program to the attorney representing the department shall be confidential and privileged as provided for in this section. Such communications shall not be disclosed to anyone other than the agency except as provided for in this section. Such disclosures shall be protected as if there were an attorney-client relationship between the attorney for the agency and the person who seeks services from the department.

(6) A discussion or activity that is not a meeting for purposes of s. 286.011 shall not be construed to waive the attorney-client privilege established in this section. This shall not be construed to constitute an exemption to either s. 119.07 or s. 286.011.

§ 90.503. Psychotherapist-patient privilege

(1) For purposes of this section:

    (a) A "psychotherapist" is:

        1. A person authorized to practice medicine in any state or nation, or reasonably believed by the patient so to be, who is engaged in the diagnosis or treatment of a mental or

       emotional condition, including alcoholism and other drug addiction;

2. A person licensed or certified as a psychologist under the laws of any state or nation, who is engaged primarily in the diagnosis or treatment of a mental or emotional condition, including alcoholism and other drug addiction;

3. A person licensed or certified as a clinical social worker, marriage and family therapist, or mental health counselor under the laws of this state, who is engaged primarily in the diagnosis or treatment of a mental or emotional condition, including alcoholism and other drug addiction;

4. Treatment personnel of facilities licensed by the state pursuant to chapter 394, chapter 395, or chapter 397, of facilities designated by the Department of Children and Families pursuant to chapter 394 as treatment facilities, or of facilities defined as community mental health centers pursuant to s. 394.907(1), who are engaged primarily in the diagnosis or treatment of a mental or emotional condition, including alcoholism and other drug addiction; or

5. An advanced practice registered nurse licensed under s. 464.012, whose primary scope of practice is the diagnosis or treatment of mental or emotional conditions, including chemical abuse, and limited only to actions performed in accordance with part I of chapter 464.

(b) A "patient" is a person who consults, or is interviewed by, a psychotherapist for purposes of diagnosis or treatment of a mental or emotional condition, including alcoholism and other drug addiction.

(c) A communication between psychotherapist and patient is "confidential" if it is not intended to be disclosed to third persons other than:

1. Those persons present to further the interest of the patient in the consultation, examination, or interview.

2. Those persons necessary for the transmission of the communication.

3. Those persons who are participating in the diagnosis and treatment under the direction of the psychotherapist.

(2) A patient has a privilege to refuse to disclose, and to prevent any other person from disclosing, confidential communications or records made for the purpose of diagnosis or treatment of the patient's mental or

emotional condition, including alcoholism and other drug addiction, between the patient and the psychotherapist, or persons who are participating in the diagnosis or treatment under the direction of the psychotherapist. This privilege includes any diagnosis made, and advice given, by the psychotherapist in the course of that relationship.

(3) The privilege may be claimed by:

    (a) The patient or the patient's attorney on the patient's behalf.

    (b) A guardian or conservator of the patient.

    (c) The personal representative of a deceased patient.

    (d) The psychotherapist, but only on behalf of the patient. The authority of a psychotherapist to claim the privilege is presumed in the absence of evidence to the contrary.

(4) There is no privilege under this section:

    (a) For communications relevant to an issue in proceedings to compel hospitalization of a patient for mental illness, if the psychotherapist in the course of diagnosis or treatment has reasonable cause to believe the patient is in need of hospitalization.

    (b) For communications made in the course of a court-ordered examination of the mental or emotional condition of the patient.

    (c) For communications relevant to an issue of the mental or emotional condition of the patient in any proceeding in which the patient relies upon the condition as an element of his or her claim or defense or, after the patient's death, in any proceeding in which any party relies upon the condition as an element of the party's claim or defense.

§ 90.5035. Sexual assault counselor-victim privilege

(1) For purposes of this section:

    (a) A "rape crisis center" is any public or private agency that offers assistance to victims of sexual assault or sexual battery and their families.

    (b) A "sexual assault counselor" is any employee of a rape crisis center whose primary purpose is the rendering of advice, counseling, or assistance to victims of sexual assault or sexual battery.

    (c) A "trained volunteer" is a person who volunteers at a rape crisis center, has completed 30 hours of training in assisting victims of sexual violence and related topics provided by the rape crisis center, is supervised by members of the staff of the rape crisis center, and is included on a list of volunteers that is maintained by the rape crisis center.

(d) A "victim" is a person who consults a sexual assault counselor or a trained volunteer for the purpose of securing advice, counseling, or assistance concerning a mental, physical, or emotional condition caused by a sexual assault or sexual battery, an alleged sexual assault or sexual battery, or an attempted sexual assault or sexual battery.

(e) A communication between a sexual assault counselor or trained volunteer and a victim is "confidential" if it is not intended to be disclosed to third persons other than:

1. Those persons present to further the interest of the victim in the consultation, examination, or interview.
2. Those persons necessary for the transmission of the communication.
3. Those persons to whom disclosure is reasonably necessary to accomplish the purposes for which the sexual assault counselor or the trained volunteer is consulted.

(2) A victim has a privilege to refuse to disclose, and to prevent any other person from disclosing, a confidential communication made by the victim to a sexual assault counselor or trained volunteer or any record made in the course of advising, counseling, or assisting the victim. Such confidential communication or record may be disclosed only with the prior written consent of the victim. This privilege includes any advice given by the sexual assault counselor or trained volunteer in the course of that relationship.

(3) The privilege may be claimed by:

(a) The victim or the victim's attorney on his or her behalf.
(b) A guardian or conservator of the victim.
(c) The personal representative of a deceased victim.
(d) The sexual assault counselor or trained volunteer, but only on behalf of the victim. The authority of a sexual assault counselor or trained volunteer to claim the privilege is presumed in the absence of evidence to the contrary.

§ 90.5036. Domestic violence advocate-victim privilege

(1) For purposes of this section:

(a) A "domestic violence center" is any public or private agency that offers assistance to victims of domestic violence, as defined in s. 741.28, and their families.

(b) A "domestic violence advocate" means any employee or volunteer who has 30 hours of training in assisting victims of domestic violence and is an employee of or volunteer for a program for victims of domestic violence whose primary purpose is the rendering of advice, counseling, or assistance to victims of domestic violence.

(c) A "victim" is a person who consults a domestic violence advocate for the purpose of securing advice, counseling, or assistance concerning a mental, physical, or emotional condition caused by an act of domestic violence, an alleged act of domestic violence, or an attempted act of domestic violence.

(d) A communication between a domestic violence advocate and a victim is "confidential" if it relates to the incident of domestic violence for which the victim is seeking assistance and if it is not intended to be disclosed to third persons other than:

    1. Those persons present to further the interest of the victim in the consultation, assessment, or interview.

    2. Those persons to whom disclosure is reasonably necessary to accomplish the purpose for which the domestic violence advocate is consulted.

(2) A victim has a privilege to refuse to disclose, and to prevent any other person from disclosing, a confidential communication made by the victim to a domestic violence advocate or any record made in the course of advising, counseling, or assisting the victim. The privilege applies to confidential communications made between the victim and the domestic violence advocate and to records of those communications only if the advocate is registered under s. 39.905 at the time the communication is made. This privilege includes any advice given by the domestic violence advocate in the course of that relationship.

(3) The privilege may be claimed by:

(a) The victim or the victim's attorney on behalf of the victim.

(b) A guardian or conservator of the victim.

(c) The personal representative of a deceased victim.

(d) The domestic violence advocate, but only on behalf of the victim. The authority of a domestic violence advocate to claim the privilege is presumed in the absence of evidence to the contrary.

§ 90.5037. Human trafficking victim advocate-victim privilege

(1) For purposes of this section, the term:
    (a) "Anti-human trafficking organization" means a registered public or private agency that offers assistance to victims of the offense of human trafficking, as defined in s. 787.06(2).
    (b) "Human trafficking victim" means a person who consults a human trafficking victim advocate or a trained volunteer for the purpose of securing advice, counseling, or services concerning a need arising from an experience of human trafficking exploitation.
    (c) "Human trafficking victim advocate" means an employee of an anti-human trafficking organization whose primary purpose is to provide advice, counseling, or services to human trafficking victims and who complies with the training requirements under subsection (5).
    (d) "Trained volunteer" means a person who volunteers with an anti-human trafficking organization and who complies with the training requirements under subsection (5).

(2) A communication between a human trafficking victim advocate or trained volunteer and a human trafficking victim is confidential if it is not intended to be disclosed to third persons other than:
    (a) Those persons present to further the interest of the human trafficking victim in the consultation, examination, or interview.
    (b) Those persons necessary for the transmission of the communication.
    (c) Those persons to whom disclosure is reasonably necessary to accomplish the purposes for which the human trafficking victim advocate or trained volunteer is consulted.

(3) A human trafficking victim has a privilege to refuse to disclose, and to prevent any other person from disclosing, a confidential communication made by the human trafficking victim to a human trafficking victim advocate or trained volunteer or a record made in the course of advising, counseling, or providing services to the human trafficking victim. Such confidential communication or record may be disclosed only with the prior written consent of the human trafficking victim. This privilege includes any advice given by the human trafficking victim advocate or trained volunteer to the human trafficking victim in the course of that relationship.

(4) The privilege may be claimed by:

(a) The human trafficking victim or the human trafficking victim's attorney on his or her behalf.

(b) The guardian or conservator of the human trafficking victim.

(c) The personal representative of a deceased human trafficking victim.

(d) The human trafficking victim advocate or trained volunteer, but only on behalf of the human trafficking victim. The authority of a human trafficking victim advocate or trained volunteer to claim the privilege is presumed in the absence of evidence to the contrary.

(5) A human trafficking victim advocate or a trained volunteer shall:

(a) Complete 24 hours of human trafficking training delivered by the Office of the Attorney General, the Bureau of Criminal Justice Programs and Victim Services, and the Florida Crime Prevention Training Institute.

(b) Within 3 years after completing the training required under paragraph (a), complete an 8-hour human trafficking update course.

§ 90.504. Husband-wife privilege

(1) A spouse has a privilege during and after the marital relationship to refuse to disclose, and to prevent another from disclosing, communications which were intended to be made in confidence between the spouses while they were husband and wife.

(2) The privilege may be claimed by either spouse or by the guardian or conservator of a spouse. The authority of a spouse, or guardian or conservator of a spouse, to claim the privilege is presumed in the absence of contrary evidence.

(3) There is no privilege under this section:

(a) In a proceeding brought by or on behalf of one spouse against the other spouse.

(b) In a criminal proceeding in which one spouse is charged with a crime committed at any time against the person or property of the other spouse, or the person or property of a child of either.

(c) In a criminal proceeding in which the communication is offered in evidence by a defendant-spouse who is one of the spouses between whom the communication was made.

§ 90.505. Privilege with respect to communications to clergy

(1) For the purposes of this section:
  (a) A "member of the clergy" is a priest, rabbi, practitioner of Christian Science, or minister of any religious organization or denomination usually referred to as a church, or an individual reasonably believed so to be by the person consulting him or her.
  (b) A communication between a member of the clergy and a person is "confidential" if made privately for the purpose of seeking spiritual counsel and advice from the member of the clergy in the usual course of his or her practice or discipline and not intended for further disclosure except to other persons present in furtherance of the communication.

(2) A person has a privilege to refuse to disclose, and to prevent another from disclosing, a confidential communication by the person to a member of the clergy in his or her capacity as spiritual adviser.

(3) The privilege may be claimed by:
  (a) The person.
  (b) The guardian or conservator of a person.
  (c) The personal representative of a deceased person.
  (d) The member of the clergy, on behalf of the person. The member of the clergy's authority to do so is presumed in the absence of evidence to the contrary.

§ 90.5055. Accountant-client privilege

(1) For purposes of this section:
  (a) An "accountant" is a certified public accountant or a public accountant.
  (b) A "client" is any person, public officer, corporation, association, or other organization or entity, either public or private, who consults an accountant with the purpose of obtaining accounting services.
  (c) A communication between an accountant and the accountant's client is "confidential" if it is not intended to be disclosed to third persons other than:
    1. Those to whom disclosure is in furtherance of the rendition of accounting services to the client.
    2. Those reasonably necessary for the transmission of the communication.

(2) A client has a privilege to refuse to disclose, and to prevent any other person from disclosing, the contents of confidential communications with an accountant when such other person learned of the communications because they were made in the rendition of accounting services to the client. This privilege includes other confidential information obtained by the accountant from the client for the purpose of rendering accounting advice.

(3) The privilege may be claimed by:

  (a) The client.

  (b) A guardian or conservator of the client.

  (c) The personal representative of a deceased client.

  (d) A successor, assignee, trustee in dissolution, or any similar representative of an organization, corporation, or association or other entity, either public or private, whether or not in existence.

  (e) The accountant, but only on behalf of the client. The accountant's authority to claim the privilege is presumed in the absence of contrary evidence.

(4) There is no accountant-client privilege under this section when:

  (a) The services of the accountant were sought or obtained to enable or aid anyone to commit or plan to commit what the client knew or should have known was a crime or fraud.

  (b) A communication is relevant to an issue of breach of duty by the accountant to the accountant's client or by the client to his or her accountant.

  (c) A communication is relevant to a matter of common interest between two or more clients, if the communication was made by any of them to an accountant retained or consulted in common when offered in a civil action between the clients.

§ 90.506. Privilege with respect to trade secrets

A person has a privilege to refuse to disclose, and to prevent other persons from disclosing, a trade secret owned by that person if the allowance of the privilege will not conceal fraud or otherwise work injustice. When the court directs disclosure, it shall take the protective measures that the interests of the holder of the privilege, the interests of the parties, and the furtherance of justice require. The privilege may be claimed by the person or the person's agent or employee.

§ 90.507. Waiver of privilege by voluntary disclosure

A person who has a privilege against the disclosure of a confidential matter or communication waives the privilege if the person, or the person's predecessor while holder of the privilege, voluntarily discloses or makes the communication when he or she does not have a reasonable expectation of privacy, or consents to disclosure of, any significant part of the matter or communication. This section is not applicable when the disclosure is itself a privileged communication.

§ 90.508. Privileged matter disclosed under compulsion or without opportunity to claim privilege

Evidence of a statement or other disclosure of privileged matter is inadmissible against the holder of the privilege if the statement or disclosure was compelled erroneously by the court or made without opportunity to claim the privilege.

§ 90.509. Application of privileged communication

Nothing in this act shall abrogate a privilege for any communication which was made prior to July 1, 1979, if such communication was privileged at the time it was made.

§ 90.510. Privileged communication necessary to adverse party

In any civil case or proceeding in which a party claims a privilege as to a communication necessary to an adverse party, the court, upon motion, may dismiss the claim for relief or the affirmative defense to which the privileged testimony would relate. In making its determination, the court may engage in an in camera inquiry into the privilege.

§ 90.601. General rule of competency

Every person is competent to be a witness, except as otherwise provided by statute.

§ 90.603. Disqualification of witness

A person is disqualified to testify as a witness when the court determines that the person is:

(1) Incapable of expressing himself or herself concerning the matter in such a manner as to be understood, either directly or through interpretation by one who can understand him or her.

(2) Incapable of understanding the duty of a witness to tell the truth.

§ 90.604. Lack of personal knowledge

Except as otherwise provided in s. 90.702, a witness may not testify to a matter unless evidence is introduced which is sufficient to support a finding that the witness has personal knowledge of the matter. Evidence to prove personal knowledge may be given by the witness's own testimony.

§ 90.605. Oath or affirmation of witness

(1) Before testifying, each witness shall declare that he or she will testify truthfully, by taking an oath or affirmation in substantially the following form: "Do you swear or affirm that the evidence you are about to give will be the truth, the whole truth, and nothing but the truth?" The witness's answer shall be noted in the record.

(2) In the court's discretion, a child may testify without taking the oath if the court determines the child understands the duty to tell the truth or the duty not to lie.

§ 90.606. Interpreters and translators

(1)

    (a) When a judge determines that a witness cannot hear or understand the English language, or cannot express himself or herself in English sufficiently to be understood, an interpreter who is duly qualified to interpret for the witness shall be sworn to do so.

    (b) This section is not limited to persons who speak a language other than English, but applies also to the language and descriptions of any person, such as a child or a person who is mentally or developmentally disabled, who cannot be reasonably understood, or who cannot understand questioning, without the aid of an interpreter.

(2) A person who serves in the role of interpreter or translator in any action or proceeding is subject to all the provisions of this chapter relating to witnesses.

(3) An interpreter shall take an oath that he or she will make a true interpretation of the questions asked and the answers given and that

the interpreter will make a true translation into English of any writing which he or she is required by his or her duties to decipher or translate.

§ 90.6063. Interpreter services for deaf persons

(1) The Legislature finds that it is an important concern that the rights of deaf citizens be protected. It is the intent of the Legislature to ensure that appropriate and effective interpreter services be made available to Florida's deaf citizens.

(2) In all judicial proceedings and in sessions of a grand jury wherein a deaf person is a complainant, defendant, witness, or otherwise a party, or wherein a deaf person is a juror or grand juror, the court or presiding officer shall appoint a qualified interpreter to interpret the proceedings or deliberations to the deaf person and to interpret the deaf person's testimony, statements, or deliberations to the court, jury, or grand jury. A qualified interpreter shall be appointed, or other auxiliary aid provided as appropriate, for the duration of the trial or other proceeding in which a deaf juror or grand juror is seated.

(3)

    (a) "Deaf person" means any person whose hearing is so seriously impaired as to prohibit the person from understanding oral communications when spoken in a normal, conversational tone.

    (b) For the purposes of this section, the term "qualified interpreter" means an interpreter certified by the National Registry of Interpreters for the Deaf or the Florida Registry of Interpreters for the Deaf or an interpreter whose qualifications are otherwise determined by the appointing authority.

(4) Every deaf person whose appearance before a proceeding entitles him or her to an interpreter shall notify the appointing authority of his or her disability not less than 5 days prior to any appearance and shall request at such time the services of an interpreter. Whenever a deaf person receives notification of the time of an appearance before a proceeding less than 5 days prior to the proceeding, the deaf person shall provide his or her notification and request as soon thereafter as practicable. In any case, nothing in this subsection shall operate to relieve an appointing authority's duty to provide an interpreter for a deaf person so entitled, and failure to strictly comply with the notice requirement will not be deemed a waiver of the right to an interpreter. An appointing authority may require a person requesting the appointment of an interpreter to furnish reasonable proof of the

person's disability when the appointing authority has reason to believe that the person is not so disabled.

(5) The appointing authority may channel requests for qualified interpreters through:

    (a) The Florida Registry of Interpreters for the Deaf;

    (b) The Division of Vocational Rehabilitation of the Department of Education; or

    (c) Any other resource wherein the appointing authority knows that qualified interpreters can be found.

(6) No qualified interpreter shall be appointed unless the appointing authority and the deaf person make a preliminary determination that the interpreter is able to communicate readily with the deaf person and is able to repeat and translate statements to and from the deaf person accurately.

(7) Before a qualified interpreter may participate in any proceedings subsequent to an appointment under the provisions of this act, such interpreter shall make an oath or affirmation that he or she will make a true interpretation in an understandable manner to the deaf person for whom the interpreter is appointed and that he or she will repeat the statements of the deaf person in the English language to the best of his or her skill and judgment. Whenever a deaf person communicates through an interpreter to any person under such circumstances that the communication would be privileged, and the recipient of the communication could not be compelled to testify as to the communication, this privilege shall apply to the interpreter.

(8) An interpreter appointed by the court in a criminal matter or in a civil matter shall be entitled to a reasonable fee for such service, in addition to actual expenses for travel, to be paid out of general county funds.

§ 90.607. Competency of certain persons as witnesses

(1)

    (a) Except as provided in paragraph (b), the judge presiding at the trial of an action is not competent to testify as a witness in that trial. An objection is not necessary to preserve the point.

    (b) By agreement of the parties, the trial judge may give evidence on a purely formal matter to facilitate the trial of the action.

(2)

    (a) A member of the jury is not competent to testify as a witness in a trial when he or she is sitting as a juror. If the juror is called to testify, the opposing party shall be given an opportunity to object out of the presence of the jury.

(b) Upon an inquiry into the validity of a verdict or indictment, a juror is not competent to testify as to any matter which essentially inheres in the verdict or indictment.

§ 90.608. Who may impeach

Any party, including the party calling the witness, may attack the credibility of a witness by:

(1) Introducing statements of the witness which are inconsistent with the witness's present testimony.

(2) Showing that the witness is biased.

(3) Attacking the character of the witness in accordance with the provisions of s. 90.609 or s. 90.610.

(4) Showing a defect of capacity, ability, or opportunity in the witness to observe, remember, or recount the matters about which the witness testified.

(5) Proof by other witnesses that material facts are not as testified to by the witness being impeached.

§ 90.609. Character of witness as impeachment

A party may attack or support the credibility of a witness, including an accused, by evidence in the form of reputation, except that:

(1) The evidence may refer only to character relating to truthfulness.

(2) Evidence of a truthful character is admissible only after the character of the witness for truthfulness has been attacked by reputation evidence.

§ 90.610. Conviction of certain crimes as impeachment

(1) A party may attack the credibility of any witness, including an accused, by evidence that the witness has been convicted of a crime if the crime was punishable by death or imprisonment in excess of 1 year under the law under which the witness was convicted, or if the crime involved dishonesty or a false statement regardless of the punishment, with the following exceptions:

(a) Evidence of any such conviction is inadmissible in a civil trial if it is so remote in time as to have no bearing on the present character of the witness.

    (b) Evidence of juvenile adjudications are inadmissible under this subsection.

(2) The pendency of an appeal or the granting of a pardon relating to such crime does not render evidence of the conviction from which the appeal was taken or for which the pardon was granted inadmissible. Evidence of the pendency of the appeal is admissible.

(3) Nothing in this section affects the admissibility of evidence under s. 90.404 or s. 90.608.

§ 90.611. Religious beliefs or opinions

Evidence of the beliefs or opinions of a witness on matters of religion is inadmissible to show that the witness's credibility is impaired or enhanced thereby.

§ 90.612. Mode and order of interrogation and presentation

(1) The judge shall exercise reasonable control over the mode and order of the interrogation of witnesses and the presentation of evidence, so as to:

    (a) Facilitate, through effective interrogation and presentation, the discovery of the truth.

    (b) Avoid needless consumption of time.

    (c) Protect witnesses from harassment or undue embarrassment.

(2) Cross-examination of a witness is limited to the subject matter of the direct examination and matters affecting the credibility of the witness. The court may, in its discretion, permit inquiry into additional matters.

(3) Leading questions should not be used on the direct examination of a witness except as may be necessary to develop the witness's testimony. Ordinarily, leading questions should be permitted on cross-examination. When a party calls a hostile witness, an adverse party, or a witness identified with an adverse party, interrogation may be by leading questions.

The judge shall take special care to protect a witness under age 14 from questions that are in a form that cannot reasonably be understood by a person of the age and understanding of the witness, and shall take special care to restrict the unnecessary repetition of questions.

§ 90.613. Refreshing the memory of a witness

When a witness uses a writing or other item to refresh memory while testifying, an adverse party is entitled to have such writing or other item produced at the hearing, to inspect it, to cross-examine the witness thereon, and to introduce it, or, in the case of a writing, to introduce those portions which relate to the testimony of the witness, in evidence. If it is claimed that the writing contains matters not related to the subject matter of the testimony, the judge shall examine the writing in camera, excise any portions not so related, and order delivery of the remainder to the party entitled thereto. Any portion withheld over objection shall be preserved and made available to the appellate court in the event of an appeal. If a writing or other item is not produced or delivered pursuant to order under this section, the testimony of the witness concerning those matters shall be stricken.

§ 90.614. Prior statements of witnesses

(1) When a witness is examined concerning the witness's prior written statement or concerning an oral statement that has been reduced to writing, the court, on motion of the adverse party, shall order the statement to be shown to the witness or its contents disclosed to him or her.

(2) Extrinsic evidence of a prior inconsistent statement by a witness is inadmissible unless the witness is first afforded an opportunity to explain or deny the prior statement and the opposing party is afforded an opportunity to interrogate the witness on it, or the interests of justice otherwise require. If a witness denies making or does not distinctly admit making the prior inconsistent statement, extrinsic evidence of such statement is admissible. This subsection is not applicable to admissions of a party-opponent as defined in s. 90.803(18).

§ 90.615. Calling witnesses by the court

(1) The court may call witnesses whom all parties may cross-examine.

(2) When required by the interests of justice, the court may interrogate witnesses, whether called by the court or by a party.

§ 90.616. Exclusion of witnesses

(1) At the request of a party the court shall order, or upon its own motion the court may order, witnesses excluded from a proceeding so that they cannot hear the testimony of other witnesses except as provided in subsection (2).

(2) A witness may not be excluded if the witness is:
    (a) A party who is a natural person.
    (b) In a civil case, an officer or employee of a party that is not a natural person. The party's attorney shall designate the officer or employee who shall be the party's representative.
    (c) A person whose presence is shown by the party's attorney to be essential to the presentation of the party's cause.
    (d) In a criminal case, the victim of the crime, the victim's next of kin, the parent or guardian of a minor child victim, or a lawful representative of such person, unless, upon motion, the court determines such person's presence to be prejudicial.

§ 90.701. Opinion testimony of lay witnesses

If a witness is not testifying as an expert, the witness's testimony about what he or she perceived may be in the form of inference and opinion when:

(1) The witness cannot readily, and with equal accuracy and adequacy, communicate what he or she has perceived to the trier of fact without testifying in terms of inferences or opinions and the witness's use of inferences or opinions will not mislead the trier of fact to the prejudice of the objecting party; and

(2) The opinions and inferences do not require a special knowledge, skill, experience, or training.

§ 90.702. Testimony by experts

If scientific, technical, or other specialized knowledge will assist the trier of fact in understanding the evidence or in determining a fact in issue, a witness qualified as an expert by knowledge, skill, experience, training, or education may testify about it in the form of an opinion or otherwise, if:

(1) The testimony is based upon sufficient facts or data;

(2) The testimony is the product of reliable principles and methods; and

(3) The witness has applied the principles and methods reliably to the facts of the case.

§ 90.703. Opinion on ultimate issue

Testimony in the form of an opinion or inference otherwise admissible is not objectionable because it includes an ultimate issue to be decided by the trier of fact.

§ 90.704. Basis of opinion testimony by experts

The facts or data upon which an expert bases an opinion or inference may be those perceived by, or made known to, the expert at or before the trial. If the facts or data are of a type reasonably relied upon by experts in the subject to support the opinion expressed, the facts or data need not be admissible in evidence. Facts or data that are otherwise inadmissible may not be disclosed to the jury by the proponent of the opinion or inference unless the court determines that their probative value in assisting the jury to evaluate the expert's opinion substantially outweighs their prejudicial effect.

§ 90.705. Disclosure of facts or data underlying expert opinion

(1) Unless otherwise required by the court, an expert may testify in terms of opinion or inferences and give reasons without prior disclosure of the underlying facts or data. On cross-examination the expert shall be required to specify the facts or data.

(2) Prior to the witness giving the opinion, a party against whom the opinion or inference is offered may conduct a voir dire examination of the witness directed to the underlying facts or data for the witness's opinion. If the party establishes prima facie evidence that the expert does not have a sufficient basis for the opinion, the opinions and inferences of the expert are inadmissible unless the party offering the testimony establishes the underlying facts or data.

§ 90.706. Authoritativeness of literature for use in cross-examination

Statements of facts or opinions on a subject of science, art, or specialized knowledge contained in a published treatise, periodical, book, dissertation, pamphlet, or other writing may be used in cross-examination of an expert witness if the expert witness recognizes the author or the treatise, periodical, book, dissertation, pamphlet, or other writing to be authoritative, or, notwithstanding nonrecognition by the expert witness, if the trial court finds the author or the treatise, periodical, book, dissertation, pamphlet, or other writing to be authoritative and relevant to the subject matter.

§ 90.801. Hearsay; definitions; exceptions

(1) The following definitions apply under this chapter:
    (a) A "statement" is:
        1. An oral or written assertion; or
        2. Nonverbal conduct of a person if it is intended by the person as an assertion.
    (b) A "declarant" is a person who makes a statement.
    (c) "Hearsay" is a statement, other than one made by the declarant while testifying at the trial or hearing, offered in evidence to prove the truth of the matter asserted.
(2) A statement is not hearsay if the declarant testifies at the trial or hearing and is subject to cross-examination concerning the statement and the statement is:
    (a) Inconsistent with the declarant's testimony and was given under oath subject to the penalty of perjury at a trial, hearing, or other proceeding or in a deposition;
    (b) Consistent with the declarant's testimony and is offered to rebut an express or implied charge against the declarant of improper influence, motive, or recent fabrication; or
    (c) One of identification of a person made after perceiving the person.

§ 90.802. Hearsay rule

Except as provided by statute, hearsay evidence is inadmissible.

§ 90.803. Hearsay exceptions; availability of declarant immaterial

The provision of s. 90.802 to the contrary notwithstanding, the following are not inadmissible as evidence, even though the declarant is available as a witness:

(1) **Spontaneous Statement**. A spontaneous statement describing or explaining an event or condition made while the declarant was perceiving the event or condition, or immediately thereafter, except when such statement is made under circumstances that indicate its lack of trustworthiness.

(2) **Excited Utterance**. A statement or excited utterance relating to a startling event or condition made while the declarant was under the stress of excitement caused by the event or condition.

(3) **Then-Existing Mental, Emotional, Or Physical Condition**.
    (a) A statement of the declarant's then-existing state of mind, emotion, or physical sensation, including a statement of intent, plan, motive, design, mental feeling, pain, or bodily health, when such evidence is offered to:
        1. Prove the declarant's state of mind, emotion, or physical sensation at that time or at any other time when such state is an issue in the action.
        2. Prove or explain acts of subsequent conduct of the declarant.
    (b) However, this subsection does not make admissible:
        1. An after-the-fact statement of memory or belief to prove the fact remembered or believed, unless such statement relates to the execution, revocation, identification, or terms of the declarant's will.
        2. A statement made under circumstances that indicate its lack of trustworthiness.

(4) **Statements for Purposes of Medical Diagnosis or Treatment**. Statements made for purposes of medical diagnosis or treatment by a person seeking the diagnosis or treatment, or made by an individual who has knowledge of the facts and is legally responsible for the person who is unable to communicate the facts, which statements describe medical history, past or present symptoms, pain, or sensations, or the inceptions or general character of the cause or external source thereof, insofar as reasonably pertinent to diagnosis or treatment.

(5) **Recorded Recollection**. A memorandum or record concerning a matter about which a witness once had knowledge, but now has insufficient recollection to enable the witness to testify fully and accurately, shown to have been made by the witness when the matter was fresh in the witness's memory and to reflect that knowledge correctly. A party may read into evidence a memorandum or record when it is admitted, but no such memorandum or record is admissible as an exhibit unless offered by an adverse party.

(6) **Records of Regularly Conducted Business Activity**.
    (a) A memorandum, report, record, or data compilation, in any form, of acts, events, conditions, opinion, or diagnosis, made at or near the time by, or from information transmitted by, a person with

knowledge, if kept in the course of a regularly conducted business activity and if it was the regular practice of that business activity to make such memorandum, report, record, or data compilation, all as shown by the testimony of the custodian or other qualified witness, or as shown by a certification or declaration that complies with paragraph (c) and s. 90.902(11), unless the sources of information or other circumstances show lack of trustworthiness. The term "business" as used in this paragraph includes a business, institution, association, profession, occupation, and calling of every kind, whether or not conducted for profit.

(b) Evidence in the form of an opinion or diagnosis is inadmissible under paragraph (a) unless such opinion or diagnosis would be admissible under ss. 90.701-90.705 if the person whose opinion is recorded were to testify to the opinion directly.

(c) A party intending to offer evidence under paragraph (a) by means of a certification or declaration shall serve reasonable written notice of that intention upon every other party and shall make the evidence available for inspection sufficiently in advance of its offer in evidence to provide to any other party a fair opportunity to challenge the admissibility of the evidence. If the evidence is maintained in a foreign country, the party intending to offer the evidence must provide written notice of that intention at the arraignment or as soon after the arraignment as is practicable or, in a civil case, 60 days before the trial. A motion opposing the admissibility of such evidence must be made by the opposing party and determined by the court before trial. A party's failure to file such a motion before trial constitutes a waiver of objection to the evidence, but the court for good cause shown may grant relief from the waiver.

(7) **Absence of Entry in Records of Regularly Conducted Activity**. Evidence that a matter is not included in the memoranda, reports, records, or data compilations, in any form, of a regularly conducted activity to prove the nonoccurrence or nonexistence of the matter, if the matter was of a kind of which a memorandum, report, record, or data compilation was regularly made and preserved, unless the sources of information or other circumstances show lack of trustworthiness.

(8) **Public Records and Reports**. Records, reports, statements reduced to writing, or data compilations, in any form, of public offices or agencies, setting forth the activities of the office or agency, or matters

observed pursuant to duty imposed by law as to matters which there was a duty to report, excluding in criminal cases matters observed by a police officer or other law enforcement personnel, unless the sources of information or other circumstances show their lack of trustworthiness. The criminal case exclusion shall not apply to an affidavit otherwise admissible under s. 316.1934 or s. 327.354.

(9) **Records Of Vital Statistics**. Records or data compilations, in any form, of births, fetal deaths, deaths, or marriages, if a report was made to a public office pursuant to requirements of law. However, nothing in this section shall be construed to make admissible any other marriage of any party to any cause of action except for the purpose of impeachment as set forth in s. 90.610.

(10) **Absence of Public Record or Entry**. Evidence, in the form of a certification in accord with s. 90.902, or in the form of testimony, that diligent search failed to disclose a record, report, statement, or data compilation or entry, when offered to prove the absence of the record, report, statement, or data compilation or the nonoccurrence or nonexistence of a matter of which a record, report, statement, or data compilation would regularly have been made and preserved by a public office and agency.

(11) **Records of Religious Organizations**. Statements of births, marriages, divorces, deaths, parentage, ancestry, relationship by blood or marriage, or other similar facts of personal or family history contained in a regularly kept record of a religious organization.

(12) **Marriage, Baptismal, and Similar Certificates**. Statements of facts contained in a certificate that the maker performed a marriage or other ceremony or administered a sacrament, when such statement was certified by a member of the clergy, public official, or other person authorized by the rules or practices of a religious organization or by law to perform the act certified, and when such certificate purports to have been issued at the time of the act or within a reasonable time thereafter.

(13) **Family Records**. Statements of fact concerning personal or family history in family Bibles, charts, engravings in rings, inscriptions on family portraits, engravings on urns, crypts, or tombstones, or the like.

(14) **Records of Documents Affecting an Interest in Property**. The record of a document purporting to establish or affect an interest in property, as proof of the contents of the original recorded or filed document and its execution and delivery by each person by whom it purports to have been executed, if the record is a record of a public

office and an applicable statute authorized the recording or filing of the document in the office.

(15) **Statements in Documents Affecting an Interest in Property**. A statement contained in a document purporting to establish or affect an interest in property, if the matter stated was relevant to the purpose of the document, unless dealings with the property since the document was made have been inconsistent with the truth of the statement or the purport of the document.

(16) **Statements in Ancient Documents**. Statements in a document in existence 20 years or more, the authenticity of which is established.

(17) **Market Reports, Commercial Publications**. Market quotations, tabulations, lists, directories, or other published compilations, generally used and relied upon by the public or by persons in particular occupations if, in the opinion of the court, the sources of information and method of preparation were such as to justify their admission.

(18) **Admissions**. A statement that is offered against a party and is:

   (a) The party's own statement in either an individual or a representative capacity;

   (b) A statement of which the party has manifested an adoption or belief in its truth;

   (c) A statement by a person specifically authorized by the party to make a statement concerning the subject;

   (d) A statement by the party's agent or servant concerning a matter within the scope of the agency or employment thereof, made during the existence of the relationship; or

   (e) A statement by a person who was a coconspirator of the party during the course, and in furtherance, of the conspiracy. Upon request of counsel, the court shall instruct the jury that the conspiracy itself and each member's participation in it must be established by independent evidence, either before the introduction of any evidence or before evidence is admitted under this paragraph.

(19) **Reputation Concerning Personal or Family History**. Evidence of reputation:

   (a) Among members of a person's family by blood, adoption, or marriage;

   (b) Among a person's associates; or

   (c) In the community,

concerning a person's birth, adoption, marriage, divorce, death, relationship by blood, adoption, or marriage, ancestry, or other similar fact of personal or family history.

(20) **Reputation Concerning Boundaries or General History**. Evidence of reputation:
   (a) In a community, arising before the controversy about the boundaries of, or customs affecting lands in, the community.
   (b) About events of general history which are important to the community, state, or nation where located.

(21) **Reputation as to Character**. Evidence of reputation of a person's character among associates or in the community.

(22) **Former Testimony**. Former testimony given by the declarant which testimony was given as a witness at another hearing of the same or a different proceeding, or in a deposition taken in compliance with law in the course of the same or another proceeding, if the party against whom the testimony is now offered, or, in a civil action or proceeding, a predecessor in interest, or a person with a similar interest, had an opportunity and similar motive to develop the testimony by direct, cross, or redirect examination; provided, however, the court finds that the testimony is not inadmissible pursuant to s. 90.402 or s. 90.403.

(23) **Hearsay Exception; Statement of Child Victim**.
   (a) Unless the source of information or the method or circumstances by which the statement is reported indicates a lack of trustworthiness, an out-of-court statement made by a child victim with a physical, mental, emotional, or developmental age of 16 or less describing any act of child abuse or neglect, any act of sexual abuse against a child, the offense of child abuse, the offense of aggravated child abuse, or any offense involving an unlawful sexual act, contact, intrusion, or penetration performed in the presence of, with, by, or on the declarant child, not otherwise admissible, is admissible in evidence in any civil or criminal proceeding if:
      1. The court finds in a hearing conducted outside the presence of the jury that the time, content, and circumstances of the statement provide sufficient safeguards of reliability. In making its determination, the court may consider the mental and physical age and maturity of the child, the nature and duration of the abuse or offense, the relationship of the child to the offender, the reliability of the assertion, the reliability

of the child victim, and any other factor deemed appropriate; and

  2. The child either:

    a. Testifies; or

    b. Is unavailable as a witness, provided that there is other corroborative evidence of the abuse or offense. Unavailability shall include a finding by the court that the child's participation in the trial or proceeding would result in a substantial likelihood of severe emotional or mental harm, in addition to findings pursuant to s. 90.804(1).

(b) In a criminal action, the defendant shall be notified no later than 10 days before trial that a statement which qualifies as a hearsay exception pursuant to this subsection will be offered as evidence at trial. The notice shall include a written statement of the content of the child's statement, the time at which the statement was made, the circumstances surrounding the statement which indicate its reliability, and such other particulars as necessary to provide full disclosure of the statement.

(c) The court shall make specific findings of fact, on the record, as to the basis for its ruling under this subsection.

(24) **Hearsay Exception; Statement of Elderly Person or Disabled Adult**.

(a) Unless the source of information or the method or circumstances by which the statement is reported indicates a lack of trustworthiness, an out-of-court statement made by an elderly person or disabled adult, as defined in s. 825.101, describing any act of abuse or neglect, any act of exploitation, the offense of battery or aggravated battery or assault or aggravated assault or sexual battery, or any other violent act on the declarant elderly person or disabled adult, not otherwise admissible, is admissible in evidence in any civil or criminal proceeding if:

  1. The court finds in a hearing conducted outside the presence of the jury that the time, content, and circumstances of the statement provide sufficient safeguards of reliability. In making its determination, the court may consider the mental and physical age and maturity of the elderly person or disabled adult, the nature and duration of the abuse or offense, the relationship of the victim to the offender, the reliability of the assertion, the reliability of the elderly person

or disabled adult, and any other factor deemed appropriate; and

2.   The elderly person or disabled adult is unavailable as a witness, provided that there is corroborative evidence of the abuse or offense. Unavailability shall include a finding by the court that the elderly person's or disabled adult's participation in the trial or proceeding would result in a substantial likelihood of severe emotional, mental, or physical harm, in addition to findings pursuant to s. 90.804(1).

(b)   In a criminal action, the defendant shall be notified no later than 10 days before the trial that a statement which qualifies as a hearsay exception pursuant to this subsection will be offered as evidence at trial. The notice shall include a written statement of the content of the elderly person's or disabled adult's statement, the time at which the statement was made, the circumstances surrounding the statement which indicate its reliability, and such other particulars as necessary to provide full disclosure of the statement.

(c)   The court shall make specific findings of fact, on the record, as to the basis for its ruling under this subsection.

§ 90.804. Hearsay exceptions; declarant unavailable

(1)   **Definition of Unavailability**. "Unavailability as a witness" means that the declarant:

(a)   Is exempted by a ruling of a court on the ground of privilege from testifying concerning the subject matter of the declarant's statement;

(b)   Persists in refusing to testify concerning the subject matter of the declarant's statement despite an order of the court to do so;

(c)   Has suffered a lack of memory of the subject matter of his or her statement so as to destroy the declarant's effectiveness as a witness during the trial;

(d)   Is unable to be present or to testify at the hearing because of death or because of then-existing physical or mental illness or infirmity; or

(e)   Is absent from the hearing, and the proponent of a statement has been unable to procure the declarant's attendance or testimony by process or other reasonable means.

However, a declarant is not unavailable as a witness if such exemption, refusal, claim of lack of memory, inability to be present, or absence is due to the procurement or wrongdoing of the party who is the proponent of his or her statement in preventing the witness from attending or testifying.

(2) **Hearsay Exceptions**. The following are not excluded under s. 90.802, provided that the declarant is unavailable as a witness:

(a) Former testimony. Testimony given as a witness at another hearing of the same or a different proceeding, or in a deposition taken in compliance with law in the course of the same or another proceeding, if the party against whom the testimony is now offered, or, in a civil action or proceeding, a predecessor in interest, had an opportunity and similar motive to develop the testimony by direct, cross, or redirect examination.

(b) Statement under belief of impending death. In a civil or criminal trial, a statement made by a declarant while reasonably believing that his or her death was imminent, concerning the physical cause or instrumentalities of what the declarant believed to be impending death or the circumstances surrounding impending death.

(c) Statement against interest. A statement which, at the time of its making, was so far contrary to the declarant's pecuniary or proprietary interest or tended to subject the declarant to liability or to render invalid a claim by the declarant against another, so that a person in the declarant's position would not have made the statement unless he or she believed it to be true. A statement tending to expose the declarant to criminal liability and offered to exculpate the accused is inadmissible, unless corroborating circumstances show the trustworthiness of the statement.

(d) Statement of personal or family history. A statement concerning the declarant's own birth, adoption, marriage, divorce, parentage, ancestry, or other similar fact of personal or family history, including relationship by blood, adoption, or marriage, even though the declarant had no means of acquiring personal knowledge of the matter stated.

(e) Statement by deceased or ill declarant similar to one previously admitted. In an action or proceeding brought against the personal representative, heir at law, assignee, legatee, devisee, or survivor of a deceased person, or against a trustee of a trust created by a deceased person, or against the assignee, committee, or guardian of a mentally incompetent person, when a declarant is unavailable as provided in paragraph (1)(d), a written or oral statement made regarding the same subject matter as another statement made by the declarant that has previously been offered by an adverse party and admitted in evidence.

(f) Statement offered against a party that wrongfully caused the declarant's unavailability. A statement offered against a party that wrongfully caused, or acquiesced in wrongfully causing, the declarant's unavailability as a witness, and did so intending that result.

§ 90.805. Hearsay within hearsay

Hearsay within hearsay is not excluded under s. 90.802, provided each part of the combined statements conforms with an exception to the hearsay rule as provided in s. 90.803 or s. 90.804.

§ 90.806. Attacking and supporting credibility of declarant

(1) When a hearsay statement has been admitted in evidence, credibility of the declarant may be attacked and, if attacked, may be supported by any evidence that would be admissible for those purposes if the declarant had testified as a witness. Evidence of a statement or conduct by the declarant at any time inconsistent with the declarant's hearsay statement is admissible, regardless of whether or not the declarant has been afforded an opportunity to deny or explain it.

(2) If the party against whom a hearsay statement has been admitted calls the declarant as a witness, the party is entitled to examine the declarant on the statement as if under cross-examination.

§ 90.901. Requirement of authentication or identification

Authentication or identification of evidence is required as a condition precedent to its admissibility. The requirements of this section are satisfied by evidence sufficient to support a finding that the matter in question is what its proponent claims.

§ 90.902. Self-authentication

(1) A document bearing:

(a) A seal purporting to be that of the United States or any state, district, commonwealth, territory, or insular possession thereof;

the Panama Canal Zone; the Trust Territory of the Pacific Islands; or a court, political subdivision, department, officer, or agency of any of them; and

(b) A signature by the custodian of the document attesting to the authenticity of the seal.

(2) A document not bearing a seal but purporting to bear a signature of an officer or employee of any entity listed in subsection (1), affixed in the officer's or employee's official capacity.

(3) An official foreign document, record, or entry that is:

(a) Executed or attested to by a person in the person's official capacity authorized by the laws of a foreign country to make the execution or attestation; and

(b) Accompanied by a final certification, as provided herein, of the genuineness of the signature and official position of:

1. The executing person; or

2. Any foreign official whose certificate of genuineness of signature and official position relates to the execution or attestation or is in a chain of certificates of genuineness of signature and official position relating to the execution or attestation.

The final certification may be made by a secretary of an embassy or legation, consul general, consul, vice consul, or consular agent of the United States or a diplomatic or consular official of the foreign country assigned or accredited to the United States. When the parties receive reasonable opportunity to investigate the authenticity and accuracy of official foreign documents, the court may order that they be treated as presumptively authentic without final certification or permit them in evidence by an attested summary with or without final certification.

(4) A copy of an official public record, report, or entry, or of a document authorized by law to be recorded or filed and actually recorded or filed in a public office, including data compilations in any form, certified as correct by the custodian or other person authorized to make the certification by certificate complying with subsection (1), subsection (2), or subsection (3) or complying with any act of the Legislature or rule adopted by the Supreme Court.

(5) Books, pamphlets, or other publications purporting to be issued by a governmental authority.

(6) Printed materials purporting to be newspapers or periodicals.

(7) Inscriptions, signs, tags, or labels purporting to have been affixed in the course of business and indicating ownership, control, or origin.

(8) Commercial papers and signatures thereon and documents relating to them, to the extent provided in the Uniform Commercial Code.

(9) Any signature, document, or other matter declared by the Legislature to be presumptively or prima facie genuine or authentic.

(10) Any document properly certified under the law of the jurisdiction where the certification is made.

(11) An original or a duplicate of evidence that would be admissible under s. 90.803(6), which is maintained in a foreign country or domestic location and is accompanied by a certification or declaration from the custodian of the records or another qualified person certifying or declaring that the record:

(a) Was made at or near the time of the occurrence of the matters set forth by, or from information transmitted by, a person having knowledge of those matters;

(b) Was kept in the course of the regularly conducted activity; and

(c) Was made as a regular practice in the course of the regularly conducted activity, provided that falsely making such a certification or declaration would subject the maker to criminal penalty under the laws of the foreign or domestic location in which the certification or declaration was signed.

(12) A legal notice published in accordance with the requirements of chapter 50 in the print edition of a qualified newspaper or on a publicly accessible website as provided in s. 50.0311.

§ 90.903. Testimony of subscribing witness unnecessary

The testimony of a subscribing witness is not necessary to authenticate a writing unless the statute requiring attestation requires it.

§ 90.91. Photographs of property wrongfully taken; use in prosecution, procedure; return of property to owner

In any prosecution for a crime involving the wrongful taking of property, a photograph of the property alleged to have been wrongfully taken may be deemed competent evidence of such property and may be admissible in the prosecution to the same extent as if such property were introduced as evidence. Such photograph shall bear a written description of the property alleged to have been wrongfully taken, the name of the owner of the property, the location where the alleged wrongful taking occurred, the name of the investigating law enforcement officer, the date the photograph was taken, and the name of the photographer. Such writing shall be made under oath by the investigating law enforcement officer, and the photograph shall be identified by the signature of the photographer. Upon the filing of such photograph and writing with the law enforcement authority or court holding such property as evidence, the property may be returned to the owner from whom the property was taken.

§ 90.951. Definitions

For purposes of this chapter:
(1) "Writings" and "recordings" include letters, words, or numbers, or their equivalent, set down by handwriting, typewriting, printing, photostating, photography, magnetic impulse, mechanical or electronic recording, or other form of data compilation, upon paper, wood, stone, recording tape, or other materials.
(2) "Photographs" include still photographs, X-ray films, videotapes, and motion pictures.
(3) An "original" of a writing or recording means the writing or recording itself, or any counterpart intended to have the same effect by a person executing or issuing it. An "original" of a photograph includes the negative or any print made from it. If data are stored in a computer or similar device, any printout or other output readable by sight and shown to reflect the data accurately is an "original."
(4) "Duplicate" includes:
   (a) A counterpart produced by the same impression as the original, from the same matrix; by means of photography, including enlargements and miniatures; by mechanical or electronic rerecording; by chemical reproduction; or by other equivalent technique that accurately reproduces the original; or
   (b) An executed carbon copy not intended by the parties to be an original.

§ 90.952. Requirement of originals

Except as otherwise provided by statute, an original writing, recording, or photograph is required in order to prove the contents of the writing, recording, or photograph.

§ 90.953. Admissibility of duplicates

A duplicate is admissible to the same extent as an original, unless:

(1) The document or writing is a negotiable instrument as defined in s. 673.1041, a security as defined in s. 678.1021, or any other writing that evidences a right to the payment of money, is not itself a security agreement or lease, and is of a type that is transferred by delivery in the ordinary course of business with any necessary endorsement or assignment.

(2) A genuine question is raised about the authenticity of the original or any other document or writing.

(3) It is unfair, under the circumstance, to admit the duplicate in lieu of the original.

§ 90.954. Admissibility of other evidence of contents

The original of a writing, recording, or photograph is not required, except as provided in s. 90.953, and other evidence of its contents is admissible when:

(1) All originals are lost or destroyed, unless the proponent lost or destroyed them in bad faith.

(2) An original cannot be obtained in this state by any judicial process or procedure.

(3) An original was under the control of the party against whom offered at a time when that party was put on notice by the pleadings or by written notice from the adverse party that the contents of such original would be subject to proof at the hearing, and such original is not produced at the hearing.

(4) The writing, recording, or photograph is not related to a controlling issue.

§ 90.955. Public records

(1) The contents of an official record or of a document authorized to be recorded or filed, and actually recorded or filed, with a governmental agency, either federal, state, county, or municipal, in a place where official records or documents are ordinarily filed, including data compilations in any form, may be proved by a copy authenticated as provided in s. 90.902, if otherwise admissible.

(2) If a party cannot obtain, by the exercise of reasonable diligence, a copy that complies with subsection (1), other evidence of the contents is admissible.

§ 90.956. Summaries

When it is not convenient to examine in court the contents of voluminous writings, recordings, or photographs, a party may present them in the form of a chart, summary, or calculation by calling a qualified witness. The party intending to use such a summary must give timely written notice of his or her intention to use the summary, proof of which shall be filed with the court, and shall make the summary and the originals or duplicates of the data from which the summary is compiled available for examination or copying, or both, by other parties at a reasonable time and place. A judge may order that they be produced in court.

§ 90.957. Testimony or written admissions of a party

A party may prove the contents of writings, recordings, or photographs by the testimony or deposition of the party against whom they are offered or by that party's written admission, without accounting for the nonproduction of the original.

§ 90.958. Functions of court and jury

(1) Except as provided in subsection (2), when the admissibility under this chapter of other evidence of the contents of writings, recordings, or photographs depends upon the existence of a preliminary fact, the question as to whether the preliminary fact exists is for the court to determine.
(2) The trier of fact shall determine whether:
  (a) The asserted writing ever existed.
  (b) Another writing, recording, or photograph produced at the trial is the original.
  (c) Other evidence of the contents correctly reflects the contents.

Chapter 92 – Witnesses, Records, and Documents

92.05 Final judgments and decrees of courts of record.

All final judgments and decrees heretofore or hereafter rendered and entered in courts of record of this state, and certified copies thereof, shall be admissible as prima facie evidence in the several courts of this state of the entry and validity of such judgments and decrees. For the purposes of this section, a court of record shall be taken and construed to mean any court other than a municipal court or the Metropolitan Court of Miami-Dade County.

92.06 Judgments and decrees of United States District Courts.

All final judgments and decrees heretofore or hereafter to be rendered and entered in the United States District Courts of this state and certified copies thereof are declared to be admissible as prima facie evidence in the several courts of this state of the entry and validity of such judgments and decrees.

92.07 Judgments and decrees of this state.

The recitals in all judgments and decrees of the Supreme Court and of the several circuit courts of this state, when such judgment or decree appears regular and has been recorded as provided by law for more than 20 years, shall be admissible in evidence as prima facie proof of the truth of the facts so recited. Either party to any suit at law or equity may offer a properly certified copy of such judgment or decree entered and recorded more than 20 years prior to the institution of the suit in which the same is offered, and such copy shall be admissible in evidence as prima facie proof of the facts in said judgment or decree set forth; provided, however, the party offering the same shall at least 10 days before the trial of the suit in which this copy is offered in evidence give notice to the opposite side of the intention to offer such copy in evidence and the purpose for which the same will be offered, and deliver with such notice a copy of the judgment or decree; provided, that nothing in this law shall render admissible in evidence any instrument of writing based on any judgment, deed of conveyance or power of attorney included in this law where any such instrument of writing has heretofore been brought in question in any action at law or in equity in any suit now pending or heretofore decided.

92.08 Deeds and powers of attorney of record for 20 years or more.

The recitals in any deed of conveyance or power of attorney shall be admissible in evidence when offered in evidence by either party to any suit at law or in equity as prima facie proof of the truth of the facts therein recited, provided such deed of conveyance or power of attorney appears regular on its face and is a muniment in the chain of title under which the party offering the deed claims, and has been recorded as provided by law for more than 20 years prior to the institution of the suit in which it is offered; and provided further, that the party offering the deed of conveyance or power of attorney for such purposes shall at least 10 days before the trial of the suit in which the said copy is offered in evidence give notice to the opposite side of the intention to offer such copy in evidence and the purpose for which the same will be offered, and deliver with such notice a copy of the deed or power of attorney. The original deed or power of attorney shall be offered unless the party offering the certified copy shall show that the original is not within the custody or control of the party offering the copy.

92.09 Effect of reversal, etc., of judgment or successful attack on deed.

No copy of a judgment or decree shall be admitted in evidence as aforesaid when it shall be made to appear that such decree has been reversed, annulled, vacated, or set aside, or that the same in collateral proceedings has been successfully attacked. No deed shall be admitted in evidence as hereinbefore provided if it shall appear that the execution or validity of said deed has been successfully attacked in any proceedings to which the grantee therein named or those or any of them holding under such grantee has been a party or parties.

92.13 Certified copies of records of certified copies.

Certified copies of the record of certified copies of deeds, mortgages, powers of attorney and other instruments referred to in s. 695.19 shall have the same effect as to notice and all other purposes whatsoever as the record of the original has or can have; and certified copies of the record of such certified copies shall be admissible and may be used in evidence in the same manner and with like effect and under the same conditions as certified copies of the record of the original instrument.

92.14 United States deeds and patents and copies thereof.

Deeds and patents issued by the United States Government and photographic copies made by authority of said government from its records thereof in the General Land Office, embracing lands in this state, and certified copies of the record thereof made in this state may be used in evidence in the courts of this state subject to the same rules that are applicable to the admission in evidence of other deeds and certified copies of the record thereof.

92.141 Law enforcement employees; travel expenses; compensation as witness.

Any employee of a law enforcement agency of a municipality or county or the state who appears as an official witness to testify at any hearing or law action in any court of this state as a direct result of his or her employment in the law enforcement agency is entitled to per diem and travel expenses at the same rate provided for state employees under s. 112.061, except that if the employee travels by privately owned vehicle he or she is entitled to such travel expenses for the actual distance traveled to and from court. In addition thereto, such employee is entitled to receive the daily witness pay, exclusive of the mileage allowance, provided by s. 92.142, except when the employee is appearing as a witness during time compensated as a part of his or her normal duties.

92.142 Witnesses; pay.

(1) Witnesses in all cases, civil and criminal, in all courts, now or hereafter created, and witnesses summoned before any arbitrator or general or special magistrate appointed by the court shall receive for each day's actual attendance $5 and also 6 cents per mile for actual distance traveled to and from the courts. A witness in a criminal case required to appear in a county other than the county of his or her residence and residing more than 50 miles from the location of the trial shall be entitled to per diem and travel expenses at the same rate provided for state employees under s. 112.061, in lieu of any other witness fee.

(2) An employee of the state who is required, as a direct result of employment, to appear as an official witness to testify in the course of any action in any court of this state, or before an administrative law judge, a hearing officer, hearing examiner, or any board or

commission of the state or of its agencies, instrumentalities, or political subdivisions, shall be considered to be on duty during such appearance and shall be entitled to per diem and travel expenses as provided in s. 112.061. Except as provided in s. 92.141 and as provided in this subsection, such employee shall be required to tender to the employing agency any witness fee and other expense reimbursement received by the employee for such appearance.

(3) Any witness subpoenaed to testify on behalf of the state in any action brought pursuant to s. 895.05 or chapter 542 who is required to travel outside his or her county of residence and more than 50 miles from his or her residence, or who is required to travel from out of state, shall be entitled to per diem and travel expenses at the same rate provided for state employees under s. 112.061 in lieu of any state witness fee.

92.143 Compensation to traffic court witnesses.

Any party who secures the attendance of a witness in traffic court shall bear all costs of calling the witness, including witness fees. If the witness is required to testify on behalf of the prosecution, the office of the state attorney of the respective judicial circuit shall pay the fees and costs of calling the witness.

92.151 Witness compensation; payment; overcharges.

Compensation shall be paid to the witness by the party in whose behalf the witness is summoned, and the prevailing party may tax the same as costs against the prevailing party's adversary; but no person shall be compelled to attend court as a witness in any civil cause unless the party in whose behalf the person is summoned shall first pay the person the amount of compensation to which he or she would be entitled for mileage and per diem for 1 day, or the same is deposited with the executive officer of said court, and the person shall not be compelled to attend thereafter unless paid in advance. But if any witness should serve without payment in advance, at the completion of his or her services the witness may exhibit his or her account for compensation, and when the same shall have been taxed and approved by the court wherein the services have been rendered, such bill shall have the force and effect of judgment and execution against the party in whose behalf the witness was summoned, and be collected by the sheriff as in other cases of execution. Any witness who shall charge and receive more than is really due shall forfeit and pay to the party injured 4 times the amount so unjustly claimed; and if the witness shall willfully make out the account for more than is lawfully due, the witness shall forfeit the compensation.

92.153 Production of documents by witnesses; reimbursement of costs.

(1) DEFINITIONS. As used in this section:
  (a) "Disinterested witness" means a person to whom a summons is issued with respect to documents involving or relating to transactions of others and who has not initiated a proceeding, is not a party to a proceeding, and is not the subject of investigation in a proceeding and who, at the time the summons is issued, is not an officer, employee, accountant, or attorney, or acting as such, for a person who has initiated, is a party to, or is the subject of investigation in a proceeding.
  (b) "Document" means any book, paper, record, or other data, or a reproduction thereof.
  (c) "Proceeding" means any civil or criminal action before a court; any investigation, inquiry, or proceeding before a grand jury, a state attorney, or a state, county, municipal, or other governmental department, division, bureau, commission or other body, or any officer thereof; any action before an officer or person authorized to issue a summons; or any administrative action authorized by law.
  (d) "Summons" means any subpoena, subpoena duces tecum, order, or other legal process which requires the production of documents.

(2) REIMBURSEMENT OF A DISINTERESTED WITNESS.
  (a) In any proceeding, a disinterested witness shall be paid for any costs the witness reasonably incurs either directly or indirectly in producing, searching for, reproducing, or transporting documents pursuant to a summons; however, the cost of documents produced pursuant to a subpoena or records request by a state attorney or public defender may not exceed 15 cents per page and $10 per hour for research or retrieval.
  (b) In a proceeding before a court or an administrative agency or officer, which is not an investigation or inquiry and which by law or rule includes the right to a public trial or hearing in the same proceeding and which involves adversary parties, responsibility for payment to the disinterested witness shall be fixed by the

court, agency, or officer before which the proceeding is pending. Payment shall be enforced by the court, agency, or officer upon motion by the disinterested witness.

(c) In all other proceedings, payment to the disinterested witness shall be made by the person or governmental authority requesting the summons. Any disinterested witness who desires reimbursement of such costs shall submit a request for reimbursement, supported by an affidavit, to the person or governmental authority responsible for payment. Payment shall be made within 30 days from the date the request is submitted. If payment is not made within such time, the witness may enforce payment by bringing a separate action in a court which has jurisdiction of the total amount of such costs and which is located in the judicial circuit where the witness resides.

92.16 Certificates of Board of Trustees of the Internal Improvement Trust Fund respecting the ownership, conveyance of, and other facts in connection with public lands.

A certificate of the Board of Trustees of the Internal Improvement Trust Fund under its official seal, with respect to the present or past ownership by the state or by the school, seminary or internal improvement funds of any lands in this state, or of the conveyance or transfer of any such lands by said Board of Trustees of the Internal Improvement Trust Fund or of the State Board of Education or other officers or boards of the state having power to convey any such lands, or any facts shown by the public records of his or her office with respect to any of such lands, or the transfer, ownership, or conveyance of the same, shall be prima facie evidence of the facts therein certified, and every such certificate shall be admissible in evidence in all of the courts of this state. All such certificates shall, without other or further proof, be admitted to record and recorded in the deed books of the respective counties of this state where the lands mentioned in such certificates lie, and the record of every such certificate shall have the same force and effect for all purposes as the record of deeds.

92.17 Effect of seal of Board of Trustees of the Internal Improvement Trust Fund.

The impression of the seal of the Board of Trustees of the Internal Improvement Trust Fund upon any deed, agreement or contract, purporting to have been made by the Board of Trustees of the Internal Improvement Trust Fund, or by the members of the State Board of Education, shall entitle the same to be received in evidence in all courts and in all proceedings in this state.

92.18 Certificate of state officer.

The certificate of any state officer, under seal of office, as to any official act occurring in the course of the official business of the office in which the state officer presides, shall be prima facie evidence of such fact.

92.19 Portions of records.

In all cases where any certified copy of any record, pleading, document, deed, conveyance, paper or instrument in writing, involving the title to real estate shall be lawfully admissible in evidence in any of the courts of this state, a certified copy of such portions of such instrument as shall contain the essential parts thereof and only such portion of the descriptive matter thereof as shall be involved in the case on trial, shall likewise be admissible in evidence; and in no case shall it be necessary to include in such certified copies descriptive matter not involved in the case in which such copy is offered in evidence.

92.20 Certificates issued under authority of Congress.

Every certificate issued under authority of the Congress and every duly certified copy thereof under the seal of the United States governmental department having the authority to issue such certified copy, relating to the grade, classification, quality or condition of agricultural products shall be accepted in any court of this state as prima facie evidence of the true grade, classification, condition or quality of such agricultural product at the time of its inspection.

92.21 Certificate as to sanitary condition of buildings.

Every owner, agent, or lessee of any building or buildings used for the purpose of providing board and lodgings for the entertainment of guests, containing 10 rooms or more, who shall have obtained and posted a certificate as provided by law, may present the same as evidence in the owner's, agent's, or lessee's defense in any suit in any of the courts in this state in which damages are claimed for injuries from alleged unsanitary conditions of said buildings and premises.

92.23 Rule of evidence in suits on fire policies for loss or damage to building.

In all suits or proceedings brought upon policies of insurance on buildings against loss or damage by fire, hereafter issued or renewed, the insurer shall not be permitted to deny that the property insured was worth, at the time of insuring it by the policy, the full sum insured therein on such property.

92.231 Expert witnesses; fee.

(1) The term "expert witness" as used herein shall apply to any witness who offers himself or herself in the trial of any action as an expert witness or who is subpoenaed to testify in such capacity before a state attorney in the investigation of a criminal matter, or before a grand jury, and who is permitted by the court to qualify and testify as such, upon any matter pending before any court.

(2) Any expert or skilled witness who shall have testified in any cause shall be allowed a witness fee including the cost of any exhibits used by such witness in an amount agreed to by the parties, and the same shall be taxed as costs. In instances where services are provided for the state, including for state-paid private court-appointed counsel, payment from state funds shall be in accordance with standards adopted by the Legislature.

(3) In a criminal case in which the state or an indigent defendant requires the services of an expert witness whose opinion is relevant to the issues of the case, the expert witness shall be compensated in accordance with standards adopted by the Legislature.

92.233 Compensation of witness summoned in two or more criminal cases.

A witness subpoenaed in two or more criminal cases pending at the same time shall be paid one charge for per diem and mileage, but when the costs are taxed against the defendant, a witness may charge the full amount in each case.

92.24 Certain tax deeds prima facie evidence of title.

All tax deeds issued under and pursuant to the provisions and in the form prescribed in and by the following acts and statutes of this state, to wit: s.

10, chapter 4888, Acts, 1901 and said section as amended by s. 1, chapter 5152, Acts, 1903; s. 577 of the General Statutes of Florida, 1906; s. 779 of the Revised General Statutes of Florida, 1920, and said section as amended by s. 12, chapter 14572, Acts, 1929; are declared to be prima facie evidence of the regularity of the proceedings from the valuation of the land described in such deeds respectively, by the assessors, to the date of the deed or deeds inclusive, and shall be so received in evidence in any and all the courts of this state, without regard to date of execution.

92.25 Records destroyed by fire; use of abstracts.

Whenever in the trial of any suit, or in any proceeding in any court of this state, it shall be made to appear that the original of any deed or other instrument of writing, or of any record of any court relating to any land, the title thereof or any interest therein being in controversy in such suit or proceeding, is lost or destroyed, or not within the power of the party to produce the same, and that the record thereof has been heretofore destroyed by fire, and that no certified copy of such record is in the possession or control of such party, it is lawful for such party, and the court shall receive as evidence, any abstract of title, or letter-press copy thereof made in the ordinary course of business prior to such loss or destruction; and it is also lawful for any such party to offer, and the court shall receive as evidence, any copy, extract or minutes from such destroyed records, or from the original thereof, which were at the date of such destruction in the possession of any person or persons then engaged in the business of making abstracts of titles for others for hire.

92.251 Uniform Foreign Depositions Law.

(1) This section may be cited as the "Uniform Foreign Depositions Law."
(2) Whenever any mandate, writ or commission is issued out of any court of record in any other state, territory, district, or foreign jurisdiction, or whenever upon notice or agreement it is required to take the testimony of a witness or witnesses in this state, witnesses may be compelled to appear and testify in the same manner and by the same process and proceeding as may be employed for the purpose of taking testimony in proceedings pending in this state.
(3) This section shall be so interpreted and construed as to effectuate its general purposes to make uniform the law of those states which enact it.

92.26 Records destroyed by fire; use of sworn copies.

A sworn copy of any writing admissible under s. 92.25 made by the person or persons having possession of such writing shall be admissible in evidence; provided, the party desiring to use such sworn copy, as aforesaid, shall have given the opposite party a reasonable opportunity to verify the correctness of such copy; and provided, that no abstract of title or letter-press copy thereof, extract or minutes or copy made admissible in evidence by this section, shall be so admitted by virtue hereof unless a copy thereof shall have been served on the opposite party, or the opposite party's attorney or counsel, at least 10 days before the same is offered in evidence. Nothing herein shall be construed to prevent the impeachment of such evidence, or its exclusion by the court for good and sufficient cause.

92.27 Records destroyed by fire; effect of abstracts in evidence.

In all cases in which any destroyed abstracts, copies, minutes, extracts, maps or plats, or copies thereof, purchased and placed in the clerk's office, as provided by law, or which are made admissible in evidence under any of the provisions of this revision, whether purchased or placed in such office or not, shall be received in evidence under this law, all deeds or other instruments of writing appearing thereby to have been executed by any person or persons, or in which they appear to have joined, shall (except as against any person or persons in actual possession of the land or lot described therein at the time of the destruction of the record of such county, claiming title thereto, otherwise than under sale for taxes or special assessments) be presumed to have been executed and acknowledged according to law; and all sales under powers, and all judgments, decrees and legal proceedings, and all sales thereunder (sale for taxes and assessments, and judgments and proceedings for the enforcement of taxes and assessments excepted) shall be presumed to be regular and correct, except as against the person or persons in this section above-mentioned and excepted.

92.28 Records destroyed by fire; land title suits; what may be received in evidence.

In all suits or proceedings concerning any land, or any estate, interest or right in, or any lien or encumbrance upon the same, when it shall be made to appear that the original of any deed, conveyance, map, plat or other written or record evidence has been lost or destroyed, or is not in the power, custody or control of the party wishing to use it on the trial to produce same, and the record thereof has been heretofore destroyed by fire, the court shall receive all such evidence as may have a bearing on the case to establish the execution or contents of any deed, conveyance, map, plat record, or other written evidence so lost or destroyed; provided, that the testimony of the parties themselves shall be received only in such cases, and subject to all the qualifications in respect to such testimony as now provided by law; and provided further, that any writing in the hands of any person or persons, which may become admissible in evidence under the provisions of this section, or any part of this law, shall be rejected and not admitted as evidence, unless the same appear upon the face thereof without erasure, blemish, alteration, interlineation or interpolation in any material part, unless the same shall be explained to the satisfaction of the court, and appear fairly and honestly made in the ordinary course of business.

92.29 Photographic or electronic copies.

Photographic reproductions or reproductions through electronic recordkeeping systems made by any federal, state, county, or municipal governmental board, department or agency, in the regular course of business, of any original record, document, paper or instrument in writing or in an electronic recordkeeping system, which is, or may be, required or authorized to be made, filed, or recorded with that board, department or agency shall in all cases and in all courts and places be admitted and received as evidence with a like force and effect as the original would be, whether the original record, document, paper, or instrument in writing or in an electronic recordkeeping system is in existence or not.

92.295 Copies of voter registration records.

Any reproduction of an original voter registration record stored pursuant to s. 98.461, whether microfilmed or maintained digitally or on electronic, magnetic, or optic media, which reproduction is certified by the supervisor of elections who is the custodian of the record, is admissible as evidence in any judicial or administrative proceeding in this state with the same effect as the original voter registration record, whether the original voter registration record exists or not.

92.30 Presumption of death; official findings.

A written finding of presumed death, made by the Secretary of the Army, the Secretary of the Navy, or other officer or employee of the United States authorized to make such findings, pursuant to the 1Federal Missing Persons Act (56 Stat. 143, 1092, and Pub. L. No. 408, Ch. 371, 2d Sess. 78th Cong.; 50 U.S.C. App. Supp. 1001-17), as now or hereafter amended, or a duly certified copy of such finding, shall be received in any court, office, or other place in this state as evidence of the death of the person therein found to be dead, and the date, circumstances, and place of the person's disappearance.

92.31 Missing persons and persons imprisoned or interned in foreign countries; official reports.

An official written report or record, or duly certified copy thereof, that a person is missing, missing in action, interned in a neutral country, or beleaguered, besieged, or captured by an enemy, or is dead, or is alive, made by any officer or employee of the United States authorized by the act referred to in s. 92.30, or by any other law of the United States to make same, shall be received in any court, office, or other place in this state as evidence that such person is missing, missing in action, interned in a neutral country, or beleaguered, besieged, or captured by an enemy, or is dead, or is alive, as the case may be.

92.32 Official findings and reports; presumption of authority to issue or execute.

For the purposes of this law, any finding, report, or record, or duly certified copy thereof, purporting to have been signed by such an officer or employee of the United States as is described above, shall prima facie be deemed to have been signed and issued by such an officer or employee pursuant to law, and the person signing same shall prima facie be deemed to have acted within the scope of the person's authority. If a copy purports to have been certified by a person authorized by law to certify the same, such certified copy shall be prima facie evidence of the person's authority so to certify.

92.33 Written statement concerning injury to person or property; furnishing copies; admission as evidence.

Every person who shall take a written statement by any injured person with respect to any accident or with respect to any injury to person or property shall, at the time of taking such statement, furnish to the person making such statement a true and complete copy thereof. Any person having taken, or having possession of any written statement or a copy of such statement, by any injured person with respect to any accident or with respect to any injury to person or property shall, at the request of the person who made such statement or his or her personal representative, furnish the person who made such statement or his or her personal representative a true and complete copy thereof. No written statement by an injured person shall be admissible in evidence or otherwise used in any manner in any civil action relating to the subject matter thereof unless it shall be made to appear that a true and complete copy thereof was furnished to the person making such statement at the time of the making thereof, or, if it shall be made to appear that thereafter a person having possession of such statement refused, upon request of the person who made the statement or his or her personal representatives, to furnish him or her a true and complete copy thereof.

92.351 Prohibition against prisoners submitting nondocumentary physical evidence without authorization of court; prisoner mailings to courts.

(1) No prisoner as defined by s. 57.085 who is a party to a judicial proceeding may submit evidence or any other item that is not in paper document form to a court or clerk of court without first obtaining authorization from the court. This prohibition includes, but is not limited to, all nondocumentary evidence or items offered in support of a motion, pleading, or other document filed with the court. This prohibition does not preclude a prisoner who is appearing in person or through counsel before a court at a trial or hearing from submitting physical evidence to the court at the appropriate time.

(2) A corrections or detention facility for prisoners may conduct a cursory examination of the outside of any package or other mailing from a prisoner to a court or clerk of court of this state to determine whether the package or mailing contains materials other than paper documents. If such package or mailing appears to contain materials other than paper documents, the facility shall refuse to forward it until the sender

presents a court order authorizing the mailing of such nondocumentary items or demonstrates that the contents are not prohibited by this section.

92.38 Comparison of disputed writings.

Comparison of a disputed writing with any writing proved to the satisfaction of the judge to be genuine, shall be permitted to be made by the witnesses; and such writings, and the evidence of witnesses respecting the same, may be submitted to the jury, or to the court in case of a trial by the court, as evidence of the genuineness, or otherwise, of the writing in dispute.

92.39 Evidence of individual's claim against the state in suits between them.

In suits between the state and individuals, no claim for a credit shall be allowed upon trial, but such as shall appear to have been presented to the Chief Financial Officer for his or her examination, and by him or her disallowed in whole or in part, unless it shall be proved to the satisfaction of the court that the defendant is, at the time of the trial, in possession of vouchers not before in the defendant's power to procure, and that the defendant was prevented from exhibiting a claim for such credit at the Chief Financial Officer's office by unavoidable accident.

92.40 Reports of building, housing, or health code violations; admissibility.

A copy of a report, notice, or citation of a violation of any building, housing, or health code by a governmental agency charged with the enforcement of such codes, certified by the agency, if otherwise material shall be admissible as evidence.

92.50 Oaths, affidavits, and acknowledgments; who may take or administer; requirements.

(1) IN THIS STATE. Oaths, affidavits, and acknowledgments required or authorized under the laws of this state (except oaths to jurors and witnesses in court and such other oaths, affidavits and acknowledgments as are required by law to be taken or administered by or before particular officers) may be taken or administered by or

before any judge, clerk, or deputy clerk of any court of record within this state, including federal courts, or before any United States commissioner or any notary public within this state. The jurat, or certificate of proof or acknowledgment, shall be authenticated by the signature and official seal of such officer or person taking or administering the same; however, when taken or administered before any judge, clerk, or deputy clerk of a court of record, the seal of such court may be affixed as the seal of such officer or person.

(2) IN OTHER STATES, TERRITORIES, AND DISTRICTS OF THE UNITED STATES. Oaths, affidavits, and acknowledgments required or authorized under the laws of this state, may be taken or administered in any other state, territory, or district of the United States, before any judge, clerk or deputy clerk of any court of record, within such state, territory, or district, having a seal, or before any notary public or justice of the peace, having a seal, in such state, territory, or district; provided, however, such officer or person is authorized under the laws of such state, territory, or district to take or administer oaths, affidavits and acknowledgments. The jurat, or certificate of proof or acknowledgment, shall be authenticated by the signature and official seal of such officer or person taking or administering the same; provided, however, when taken or administered by or before any judge, clerk, or deputy clerk of a court of record, the seal of such court may be affixed as the seal of such officer or person.

(3) IN FOREIGN COUNTRIES. Oaths, affidavits, and acknowledgments, required or authorized by the laws of this state, may be taken or administered in any foreign country, by or before any judge or justice of a court of last resort, any notary public of such foreign country, any minister, consul general, charge d'affaires, or consul of the United States resident in such country. The jurat, or certificate of proof or acknowledgment, shall be authenticated by the signature and official seal of the officer or person taking or administering the same; provided, however, when taken or administered by or before any judge or justice of a court of last resort, the seal of such court may be affixed as the seal of such judge or justice.

92.51 Oaths, affidavits, and acknowledgments; taken or administered by commissioned officer of United States Armed Forces.

(1) Oaths, affidavits, and acknowledgments required or authorized by the laws of this state may be taken or administered within or without the United States by or before any commissioned officer in active service of the Armed Forces of the United States with the rank of second lieutenant or higher in the Army, Air Force or Marine Corps or ensign or higher in the Navy or Coast Guard when the person required or authorized to make and execute the oath, affidavit, or acknowledgment is a member of the Armed Forces of the United States, the spouse of such member or a person whose duties require the person's presence with the Armed Forces of the United States.

(2) A certificate endorsed upon the instrument which shows the date of the oath, affidavit, or acknowledgment and which states in substance that the person appearing before the officer acknowledged the instrument as the person's act or made or signed the instrument under oath shall be sufficient for all intents and purposes. The instrument shall not be rendered invalid by the failure to state the place of execution or acknowledgment.

(3) If the signature, rank, and branch of service or subdivision thereof of any commissioned officer appears upon such instrument, document or certificate no further proof of the authority of such officer so to act shall be required and such action by such commissioned officer shall be prima facie evidence that the person making such oath, affidavit or acknowledgment is within the purview of this act.

92.52 Affirmation equivalent to oath.

Whenever an oath shall be required by any law of this state in any proceeding, an affirmation may be substituted therefor.

92.525 Verification of documents; perjury by false written declaration, penalty.

(1) If authorized or required by law, by rule of an administrative agency, or by rule or order of court that a document be verified by a person, the verification may be accomplished in the following manner:
   (a) Under oath or affirmation taken or administered before an officer authorized under s. 92.50 to administer oaths;

   (b) Under oath or affirmation taken or administered by an officer authorized under s. 117.10 to administer oaths; or

   (c) By the signing of the written declaration prescribed in subsection (2).

(2) A written declaration means the following statement: "Under penalties of perjury, I declare that I have read the foregoing [document] and that the facts stated in it are true," followed by the signature of the person making the declaration, except when a verification on information or belief is permitted by law, in which case the words "to the best of my knowledge and belief" may be added. The written declaration shall be printed or typed at the end of or immediately below the document being verified and above the signature of the person making the declaration.

(3) A person who knowingly makes a false declaration under subsection (2) is guilty of the crime of perjury by false written declaration, a felony of the third degree, punishable as provided in s. 775.082, s. 775.083, or s. 775.084.

(4) As used in this section:

   (a) The term "administrative agency" means any department or agency of the state or any county, municipality, special district, or other political subdivision.

   (b) The term "document" means any writing including, without limitation, any form, application, claim, notice, tax return, inventory, affidavit, pleading, or paper.

   (c) The requirement that a document be verified means that the document must be signed or executed by a person and that the person must state under oath or affirm that the facts or matters stated or recited in the document are true, or words of that import or effect.

92.53 Videotaping the testimony of a victim or witness under age 18 or who has an intellectual disability.

(1) On motion and hearing in camera and a finding that there is a substantial likelihood that a victim or witness who is under the age of 18 or who has an intellectual disability as defined in s. 393.063 would suffer at least moderate emotional or mental harm due to the presence of the defendant if such victim or witness is required to testify in open court, or is unavailable as defined in s. 90.804(1), the trial court may

order the videotaping of the testimony of the victim or witness in a case, whether civil or criminal in nature, in which videotaped testimony is to be used at trial in lieu of trial testimony in open court.

(2) The motion may be filed by:

    (a) The victim or witness, or the victim's or witness's attorney, parent, legal guardian, or guardian ad litem;

    (b) A trial judge on his or her own motion;

    (c) Any party in a civil proceeding; or

    (d) The prosecuting attorney or the defendant, or the defendant's counsel.

(3) The judge shall preside, or shall appoint a special master to preside, at the videotaping unless:

    (a) The child or the person who has the intellectual disability is represented by a guardian ad litem or counsel;

    (b) The representative of the victim or witness and the counsel for each party stipulate that the requirement for the presence of the judge or special master may be waived; and

    (c) The court finds at a hearing on the motion that the presence of a judge or special master is not necessary to protect the victim or witness.

(4) The defendant and the defendant's counsel must be present at the videotaping unless the defendant has waived this right. The court may require the defendant to view the testimony from outside the presence of the child or the person who has an intellectual disability by means of a two-way mirror or another similar method that ensures that the defendant can observe and hear the testimony of the victim or witness in person, but the victim or witness cannot hear or see the defendant. The defendant and the attorney for the defendant may communicate by any appropriate private method.

(5) Any party, or the court on its own motion, may request the aid of an interpreter, as provided in s. 90.606, to aid the parties in formulating methods of questioning the child or person who has the intellectual disability and in interpreting the answers of the child or person during proceedings conducted under this section.

(6) The motion referred to in subsection (1) may be made at any time with reasonable notice to each party to the cause, and videotaping of testimony may be made any time after the court grants the motion. The videotaped testimony is admissible as evidence in the trial of the cause; however, such testimony is not admissible in any trial or

proceeding in which such witness testifies by use of closed-circuit television pursuant to s. 92.54.

(7) The court shall make specific findings of fact, on the record, as to the basis for its ruling under this section.

92.54 Use of closed-circuit television in proceedings involving a victim or witness under the age of 18 or who has an intellectual disability.

(1) Upon motion and hearing in camera and upon a finding that there is a substantial likelihood that a victim or witness under the age of 18 or who has an intellectual disability will suffer at least moderate emotional or mental harm due to the presence of the defendant if such victim or witness is required to testify in open court, or is unavailable as defined in s. 90.804(1), the trial court may order that the testimony of the victim or witness be taken outside of the courtroom and shown by means of closed-circuit television.

(2) The motion may be filed by the victim or witness; the attorney, parent, legal guardian, or guardian ad litem of the victim or witness; the prosecutor; the defendant or the defendant's counsel; or the trial judge on his or her own motion.

(3) Only the judge, the prosecutor, the defendant, the attorney for the defendant, the operators of the videotape equipment, an interpreter, and some other person who, in the opinion of the court, contributes to the well-being of the child or the person who has an intellectual disability and who will not be a witness in the case may be in the room during the recording of the testimony.

(4) During the victim's or witness's testimony by closed-circuit television, the court may require the defendant to view the testimony from the courtroom. In such a case, the court shall permit the defendant to observe and hear the testimony of the victim or witness, but must ensure that the victim or witness cannot hear or see the defendant. The defendant's right to assistance of counsel, which includes the right to immediate and direct communication with counsel conducting cross-examination, must be protected and, upon the defendant's request, such communication must be provided by any appropriate electronic method.

(5) The court shall make specific findings of fact, on the record, as to the basis for its ruling under this section.

92.55 Judicial or other proceedings involving victim or witness under the age of 18, a person who has an intellectual disability, or a sexual offense victim or witness; special protections; use of therapy animals or facility dogs.

(1) For purposes of this section, the term:
  (a) "Sexual offense victim or witness" means a person who was under the age of 18 when he or she was the victim of or a witness to a sexual offense.
  (b) "Sexual offense" means any offense specified in s. 775.21(4)(a)1. or s. 943.0435(1)(h)1.a.(I).

(2) Upon motion of any party, upon motion of a parent, guardian, attorney, guardian ad litem, or other advocate appointed by the court under s. 914.17 for a victim or witness under the age of 18, a person who has an intellectual disability, or a sexual offense victim or witness, or upon its own motion, the court may enter any order necessary to protect the victim or witness in any judicial proceeding or other official proceeding from severe emotional or mental harm due to the presence of the defendant if the victim or witness is required to testify in open court. Such orders must relate to the taking of testimony and include, but are not limited to:
  (a) Interviewing or the taking of depositions as part of a civil or criminal proceeding.
  (b) Examination and cross-examination for the purpose of qualifying as a witness or testifying in any proceeding.
  (c) The use of testimony taken outside of the courtroom, including proceedings under ss. 92.53 and 92.54.

(3) In ruling upon the motion, the court shall consider:
  (a) The age of the child, the nature of the offense or act, the relationship of the child to the parties in the case or to the defendant in a criminal action, the degree of emotional trauma that will result to the child as a consequence of the defendant's presence, and any other fact that the court deems relevant;
  (b) The age of the person who has an intellectual disability, the functional capacity of such person, the nature of the offenses or act, the relationship of the person to the parties in the case or to the defendant in a criminal action, the degree of emotional trauma

        that will result to the person as a consequence of the defendant's presence, and any other fact that the court deems relevant; or

(c) The age of the sexual offense victim or witness when the sexual offense occurred, the relationship of the sexual offense victim or witness to the parties in the case or to the defendant in a criminal action, the degree of emotional trauma that will result to the sexual offense victim or witness as a consequence of the defendant's presence, and any other fact that the court deems relevant.

(4) In addition to such other relief provided by law, the court may enter orders limiting the number of times that a child, a person who has an intellectual disability, or a sexual offense victim or witness may be interviewed, prohibiting depositions of the victim or witness, requiring the submission of questions before the examination of the victim or witness, setting the place and conditions for interviewing the victim or witness or for conducting any other proceeding, or permitting or prohibiting the attendance of any person at any proceeding. The court shall enter any order necessary to protect the rights of all parties, including the defendant in any criminal action.

(5) The court may set any other conditions it finds just and appropriate when taking the testimony of a victim or witness under the age of 18, a person who has an intellectual disability, or a sexual offense victim or witness, including the use of a therapy animal or facility dog, in any proceeding involving a sexual offense or child abuse, abandonment, or neglect.

(a) When deciding whether to permit a victim or witness under the age of 18, a person who has an intellectual disability, or a sexual offense victim or witness to testify with the assistance of a therapy animal or facility dog, the court shall consider the age of the child victim or witness, the age of the sexual offense victim or witness at the time the sexual offense occurred, the interests of the child victim or witness or sexual offense victim or witness, the rights of the parties to the litigation, and any other relevant factor that would facilitate the testimony by the victim or witness under the age of 18, person who has an intellectual disability, or sexual offense victim or witness.

(b) For purposes of this subsection the term:

1. "Facility dog" means a dog that has been trained, evaluated, and certified as a facility dog pursuant to industry standards and provides unobtrusive emotional support to children and adults in facility settings.
2. "Therapy animal" means an animal that has been trained, evaluated, and certified as a therapy animal pursuant to industry standards by an organization that certifies animals as appropriate to provide animal therapy.

92.56 Judicial proceedings and court records involving sexual offenses and human trafficking.

(1)

(a) The confidential and exempt status of criminal intelligence information or criminal investigative information made confidential and exempt pursuant to s. 119.071(2)(h) must be maintained in court records pursuant to s. 119.0714(1)(h) and in court proceedings, including testimony from witnesses.

(b) If a petition for access to such confidential and exempt records is filed with the trial court having jurisdiction over the alleged offense, the confidential and exempt status of such information shall be maintained by the court if the state or the victim demonstrates that:

1. The identity of the victim is not already known in the community;
2. The victim has not voluntarily called public attention to the offense;
3. The identity of the victim has not otherwise become a reasonable subject of public concern;
4. The disclosure of the victim's identity would be offensive to a reasonable person; and
5. The disclosure of the victim's identity would:
   a. Endanger the victim because the assailant has not been apprehended and is not otherwise known to the victim;
   b. Endanger the victim because of the likelihood of retaliation, harassment, or intimidation;
   c. Cause severe emotional or mental harm to the victim;
   d. Make the victim unwilling to testify as a witness; or
   e. Be inappropriate for other good cause shown.

(2) A defendant charged with a crime described in s. 787.06(3)(a)1., (c)1., or (e)1., s. 787.06(3)(b), (d), (f), or (g), chapter 794, or chapter 800, or with child abuse, aggravated child abuse, or sexual performance by a child as described in chapter 827, may apply to the trial court for an order of disclosure of information in court records held confidential and exempt pursuant to s. 119.0714(1)(h) or maintained as confidential and exempt pursuant to court order under this section. Such identifying information concerning the victim may be released to the defendant or his or her attorney in order to prepare the defense. The confidential and exempt status of this information may not be construed to prevent the disclosure of the victim's identity to the defendant; however, the defendant may not disclose the victim's identity to any person other than the defendant's attorney or any other person directly involved in the preparation of the defense. A willful and knowing disclosure of the identity of the victim to any other person by the defendant constitutes contempt.

(3) The state may use a pseudonym instead of the victim's name to designate the victim of a crime described in s. 787.06(3)(a)1., (c)1., or (e)1., in s. 787.06(3)(b), (d), (f), or (g), or in chapter 794 or chapter 800, or of child abuse, aggravated child abuse, or sexual performance by a child as described in chapter 827, or any crime involving the production, possession, or promotion of child pornography as described in chapter 847, in all court records and records of court proceedings, both civil and criminal.

(4) The protection of this section may be waived by the victim of the alleged offense in a writing filed with the court, in which the victim consents to the use or release of identifying information during court proceedings and in the records of court proceedings.

(5) This section does not prohibit the publication or broadcast of the substance of trial testimony in a prosecution for an offense described in s. 787.06(3)(a)1., (c)1., or (e)1., s. 787.06(3)(b), (d), (f), or (g), chapter 794, or chapter 800, or a crime of child abuse, aggravated child abuse, or sexual performance by a child, as described in chapter 827, but the publication or broadcast may not include an identifying photograph, an identifiable voice, or the name or address of the victim, unless the victim has consented in writing to the publication and filed such consent with the court or unless the court has declared such records not confidential and exempt as provided for in subsection (1).

(6) A willful and knowing violation of this section or a willful and knowing failure to obey any court order issued under this section constitutes contempt.

92.561 Prohibition on reproduction of child pornography.

(1) In a criminal proceeding, any property or material that portrays sexual performance by a child as defined in s. 827.071, or constitutes child pornography as defined in s. 847.001, must remain secured or locked in the care, custody, and control of a law enforcement agency, the state attorney, or the court.

(2) Notwithstanding any law or rule of court, a court shall deny, in a criminal proceeding, any request by the defendant to copy, photograph, duplicate, or otherwise reproduce any property or material that portrays sexual performance by a child or constitutes child pornography so long as the state attorney makes the property or material reasonably available to the defendant.

(3) For purposes of this section, property or material is deemed to be reasonably available to the defendant if the state attorney provides ample opportunity at a designated facility for the inspection, viewing, and examination of the property or material that portrays sexual performance by a child or constitutes child pornography by the defendant, his or her attorney, or any individual whom the defendant uses as an expert during the discovery process or at a court proceeding.

92.565 Admissibility of confession in sexual abuse cases.

(1) As used in this section, the term "sexual abuse" means an act of a sexual nature or sexual act that may be prosecuted under any law of this state, including those offenses specifically designated in subsection (2).

(2) In any criminal action in which the defendant is charged with a crime against a victim under s. 787.06(3), involving commercial sexual activity; s. 794.011; s. 794.05; s. 800.04; s. 826.04; s. 827.03, involving sexual abuse; s. 827.04, involving sexual abuse; s. 827.071; or s. 847.0135(5), or any other crime involving sexual abuse of another, or with any attempt, solicitation, or conspiracy to commit any of these crimes, the defendant's memorialized confession or admission is admissible during trial without the state having to prove a corpus delicti of the crime if the court finds in a hearing conducted outside the

presence of the jury that the state is unable to show the existence of each element of the crime, and having so found, further finds that the defendant's confession or admission is trustworthy. Factors which may be relevant in determining whether the state is unable to show the existence of each element of the crime include, but are not limited to, the fact that, at the time the crime was committed, the victim was:

(a) Physically helpless, mentally incapacitated, or mentally defective, as those terms are defined in s. 794.011;

(b) Physically incapacitated due to age, infirmity, or any other cause; or

(c) Less than 12 years of age.

(3) Before the court admits the defendant's confession or admission, the state must prove by a preponderance of evidence that there is sufficient corroborating evidence that tends to establish the trustworthiness of the statement by the defendant. Hearsay evidence is admissible during the presentation of evidence at the hearing. In making its determination, the court may consider all relevant corroborating evidence, including the defendant's statements.

(4) The court shall make specific findings of fact, on the record, for the basis of its ruling.

92.57 Termination of employment of witness prohibited.

A person who testifies in a judicial proceeding in response to a subpoena may not be dismissed from employment because of the nature of the person's testimony or because of absences from employment resulting from compliance with the subpoena. In any civil action arising out of a violation of this section, the court may award attorney's fees and punitive damages to the person unlawfully dismissed, in addition to actual damages suffered by such person.

92.60 Foreign records of regularly conducted business activity.

(1) For the purposes of this section:

(a) "Foreign record of regularly conducted business activity" means a memorandum, report, record, or data compilation, in any form, of acts, events, conditions, opinions, or diagnoses, maintained in a foreign country.

(b) "Foreign certification" means a written declaration made and signed in a foreign country by the custodian of a foreign record of regularly conducted business activity or another qualified person that, if falsely made, would subject the maker to criminal penalty under the laws of that country.

(c) "Business" means any business, institution, association, profession, occupation, or calling of any kind, whether or not conducted for profit.

(2) In a criminal or civil proceeding in a court of the State of Florida, a foreign record of regularly conducted business activity, or a copy of such record, shall not be excluded as evidence by the hearsay rule if a foreign certification attests that:

(a) Such record was made at or near the time of the occurrence of the matters set forth by, or from information transmitted by, a person with knowledge of those matters;

(b) Such record was kept in the course of a regularly conducted business activity;

(c) The business activity made such a record as a regular practice; and

(d) If such record is not the original, it is a duplicate of the original; unless the source of information or the method or circumstances of preparation indicate lack of trustworthiness.

(3) A foreign certification under this section shall authenticate such record or duplicate.

(4) No evidence in such records in the form of opinion or diagnosis is admissible under subsection (2) unless such opinion or diagnosis would be admissible under ss. 90.701-90.705 if the person whose opinion is recorded were to testify to the opinion directly.

(5) At the arraignment or as soon after the arraignment as practicable, or 60 days prior to a civil trial, a party intending to offer in evidence under this section a foreign record of regularly conducted business activity shall provide written notice of that intention to each other party. A motion opposing admission in evidence of such record shall be made by the opposing party and determined by the court before trial. Failure by a party to file such motion before trial shall constitute a waiver of objection to such record or duplicate, but the court for cause shown may grant relief from the waiver.

92.605 Production of certain records by Florida businesses and out-of-state corporations.

(1) For the purposes of this section, the term:

(a) "Adverse result" includes one of the following consequences to notification of the existence of a court order, a subpoena, or a search warrant:

1.   Danger to the life or physical safety of an individual.
2.   A flight from prosecution.
3.   The destruction of or tampering with evidence.
4.   The intimidation of potential witnesses.
5.   Serious jeopardy to an investigation or undue delay of a trial.

(b) "Applicant" means a law enforcement officer who is seeking a court order or subpoena under s. 16.56, s. 27.04, s. 905.185, or s. 914.04 or who is issued a search warrant under s. 933.01, or anyone who is authorized to issue a subpoena under the Florida Rules of Criminal Procedure.

(c) "Business" means any business, institution, association, profession, occupation, or calling of any kind, whether or not conducted for profit.

(d) "Electronic communication services" and "remote computing services" have the same meaning as provided in the Electronic Communications Privacy Act in chapter 121 (commencing with s. 2701) of part I of Title 18 of the United States Code Annotated. This section does not apply to corporations that do not provide those services to the public.

(e) "Out-of-state corporation" means any corporation that is qualified to do business in this state under s. 607.1501.

(f) "Out-of-state record of regularly conducted business activity" means a memorandum, report, record, or data compilation, in any form, of acts, events, conditions, opinions, or diagnoses, maintained in another state or country.

(g) "Out-of-state certification" means a written declaration made and signed in another state or country by the custodian of an out-of-state record of regularly conducted business activity or another qualified person that, if falsely made, would subject the declarant to criminal penalty under the laws of another state or country.

(h) "Properly served" means delivery by hand or in a manner reasonably allowing for proof of delivery if delivered by United States mail, overnight delivery service, or facsimile to a person or entity properly registered to do business in any state. In order for an out-of-state corporation to be properly served, the service described in this paragraph must be effected on the corporation's registered agent.

(2) The following provisions apply to any subpoena, court order, or search warrant issued in compliance with the Electronic Communications Privacy Act in chapter 121 (commencing with s. 2701) of part I of Title 18 of the United States Code and that is subject to this chapter, which allows a search for records that are in the actual or constructive possession of an out-of-state corporation that provides electronic communication services or remote computing services to the public, when those records would reveal the identity of the customers using those services; data stored by, or on behalf of, the customers; the customers' usage of those services; or the recipients or destinations of communications sent to or from those customers.

(a) Any subpoena, court order, or warrant issued under this subsection must contain the following language in bold type on the first page of the document: "This (subpoena, order, warrant) is issued pursuant to Florida Statute s. 92.605. A response is due within 20 business days of receipt of this (subpoena, order, warrant) unless a longer time period is stated herein."

(b) When properly served with a subpoena, court order, or search warrant issued by a Florida court or other applicant, an out-of-state corporation subject to this section shall provide to the applicant all records sought pursuant to such subpoena, court order, or warrant within 20 business days after receipt, or the date indicated within the subpoena, if later, including those records maintained or located outside the State of Florida. If the records cannot be produced within the 20-day time period, the out-of-state corporation shall notify the applicant within the 20-day time period and agree to produce the documents at the earliest possible time. The applicant shall pay the out-of-state corporation the reasonable expenses associated with compliance.

(c) When the applicant makes a showing and the court finds that failure to produce records within 20 business days would cause an adverse result, the subpoena, court order, or warrant may require production of records within less than 20 business days. A court may reasonably extend the time required for production of the records upon finding that the out-of-state corporation needs the extension and that an extension of time would not cause an adverse result.

(d) An out-of-state corporation seeking to quash or object to the subpoena, court order, or warrant must seek relief from the court issuing such subpoena, court order, or warrant within the time required for production of records under this section. The issuing court shall hear and decide that motion within 5 court days after the motion is filed.

(e) Upon written request from the applicant or if ordered by the court, the out-of-state corporation shall verify the authenticity of records that it produces by providing an affidavit that complies with the requirements set forth in this section. Records produced in compliance with this section are admissible in evidence as set forth in subsection (5).

(3) A Florida business that provides electronic communication services or remote computing services to the public, when served with a subpoena, court order, or warrant issued by another state to produce records that would reveal the identity of the customers using those services; data stored by, or on behalf of, the customers; the customers' usage of those services; or the recipients or destinations of communications sent to or from those customers shall produce those records as if that subpoena, court order, or warrant had been issued by a Florida court.

(4) A cause of action does not arise against any out-of-state corporation or Florida business subject to this section, or its officers, employees, agents, or other specified persons, for providing records, information, facilities, or assistance in accordance with the terms of a subpoena, court order, or warrant subject to this section.

(5) In a criminal proceeding in a court of this state, an out-of-state record of regularly conducted business activity, or a copy of such record, shall not be excluded as hearsay evidence by s. 90.802, if an out-of-state certification attests that:

(a) Such record was made at or near the time of the occurrence of the matters set forth by, or from information transmitted by, a person with knowledge of those matters.

(b) Such record was kept in the course of a regularly conducted business activity.

(c) The business activity made such a record as a regular practice.

(d) If such record is not the original, it is a duplicate of the original, unless the source of information or the method or circumstances of preparation indicate lack of trustworthiness.

(6) An out-of-state certification under this section shall authenticate such record or duplicate.

(7) No evidence in such records in the form of opinion or diagnosis is admissible under subsection (5) unless such opinion or diagnosis would be admissible under ss. 90.701-90.705 if the person whose opinion is recorded were to testify to the opinion directly.

(8) As soon after the arraignment as practicable, or 60 days prior to trial, a party intending to offer in evidence under this section an out-of-state record of regularly conducted business activity shall provide written notice of that intention to each other party. A motion opposing admission in evidence of such record shall be made by the opposing party and determined by the court before trial. Failure by a party to file such motion before trial shall constitute a waiver of objection to such record or duplicate, but the court for cause shown may grant relief from the waiver.

(9) In any criminal case, the content of any electronic communication may be obtained under this section only by court order or by the issuance of a search warrant, unless otherwise provided under the Electronic Communications Privacy Act or other provision of law.

92.70 Eyewitness identification.

(1) SHORT TITLE. This section may be cited as the "Eyewitness Identification Reform Act."

(2) DEFINITIONS. As used in this section, the term:
    (a) "Eyewitness" means a person whose identification by sight of another person may be relevant in a criminal proceeding.
    (b) "Independent administrator" means a person who is not participating in the investigation of a criminal offense and is unaware of which person in the lineup is the suspect.
    (c) "Lineup" means a photo lineup or live lineup.
    (d) "Lineup administrator" means the person who conducts a lineup.
    (e) "Live lineup" means a procedure in which a group of people is displayed to an eyewitness for the purpose of determining if the eyewitness can identify the perpetrator of a crime.
    (f) "Photo lineup" means a procedure in which an array of photographs is displayed to an eyewitness for the purpose of determining if the eyewitness can identify the perpetrator of a crime.

(3) EYEWITNESS IDENTIFICATION PROCEDURES. A lineup conducted in this state by a state, county, municipal, or other law enforcement agency must meet all of the following requirements:

(a) The lineup must be conducted by an independent administrator. However, in lieu of using an independent administrator, a law enforcement agency may conduct a photo lineup eyewitness identification procedure using an alternative method specified in subparagraph 1., subparagraph 2., or subparagraph 3. Any alternative method must be carefully structured to achieve neutral administration and to prevent the lineup administrator from knowing which photograph is being presented to the eyewitness during the identification procedure. Alternative methods may include any of the following:

   1. An automated computer program that can automatically administer the photo lineup directly to an eyewitness and prevent the lineup administrator from seeing which photograph the eyewitness is viewing until after the procedure is completed.

   2. A procedure in which photographs are placed in folders, randomly numbered, and shuffled and then presented to an eyewitness such that the lineup administrator cannot see or track which photograph is being presented to the eyewitness until after the procedure is completed.

   3. Any other procedure that achieves neutral administration and prevents the lineup administrator from knowing which photograph is being presented to the eyewitness during the identification procedure.

(b) Before a lineup, the eyewitness must be instructed that:

   1. The perpetrator might or might not be in the lineup;

   2. The lineup administrator does not know the suspect's identity, except that this instruction need not be given when a specified and approved alternative method of neutral administration is used;

   3. The eyewitness should not feel compelled to make an identification;

   4. It is as important to exclude innocent persons as it is to identify the perpetrator; and

   5. The investigation will continue with or without an identification.

The eyewitness shall acknowledge, in writing, having received a copy of the lineup instructions. If the eyewitness refuses to sign a document acknowledging receipt of the instructions, the lineup administrator must document the refusal of the eyewitness to sign a document acknowledging receipt of the instructions, and the lineup administrator must sign the acknowledgment document himself or herself.

(4) REMEDIES. All of the following remedies are available as consequences of compliance or noncompliance with any requirement of this section:

(a)

    1.   A failure on the part of a person to comply with any requirement of this section shall be considered by the court when adjudicating motions to suppress eyewitness identification.

    2.   A failure on the part of a person to comply with any requirement of this section is admissible in support of a claim of eyewitness misidentification, as long as such evidence is otherwise admissible.

(b) If evidence of compliance or noncompliance with any requirement of this section is presented at trial, the jury shall be instructed that the jury may consider credible evidence of compliance or noncompliance to determine the reliability of eyewitness identifications.

(5) EDUCATION AND TRAINING. The Criminal Justice Standards and Training Commission, in consultation with the Department of Law Enforcement, shall create educational materials and provide training programs on how to conduct lineups in compliance with this section.